THE BASEBALL
HALL OF SHAME
2

Books by Bruce Nash and Allan Zullo

The Baseball Hall of Shame
The Baseball Hall of Shame 2

Published by POCKET BOOKS

Most Pocket Books are available at special quantity discounts for bulk purchases for sales promotions, premiums or fund raising. Special books or book excerpts can also be created to fit specific needs.

For details write the office of the Vice President of Special Markets, Pocket Books, 1230 Avenue of the Americas, New York, New York 10020.

THE BASEBALL
HALL OF SHAME
2

Bruce Nash and Allan Zullo
Bernie Ward, Curator

PUBLISHED BY POCKET BOOKS NEW YORK

Another *Original* publication of POCKET BOOKS

POCKET BOOKS, a division of Simon & Schuster, Inc.
1230 Avenue of the Americas, New York, N.Y. 10020

ISBN: 0-671-61113-5

First Pocket Books trade paperback printing March, 1986

10 9 8 7 6 5 4 3 2 1

POCKET and colophon are registered trademarks of Simon & Schuster, Inc.

THE BASEBALL HALL OF SHAME is a registered trademark of Nash and Zullo
Productions, Inc.

Interior design by Barbara Cohen

PRINTED IN THE U.S.A.

*This book is dedicated to all the major league players,
managers, coaches, owners, personnel, and fans
who are big enough to laugh at their own foul-ups . . .
and to Harry Heitman, wherever you are.*

Many of today's older teams had different names in the 1890s and the early part of this century. In recounting incidents that occurred back then, we refer to these teams by their current names rather than their past monikers to avoid confusion.

Acknowledgment

We wish to thank all the fans, players, sportswriters, and broadcasters who contributed nominations.

We are especially grateful to those players, past and present, who shared a few laughs with us as they recounted the inglorious moments that earned them their niches in The Baseball Hall of SHAME.

We want to give special thanks to Al Kermisch for his outstanding research work. We also appreciate the efforts of: Rodney Beck, Phil Bergen, George Castle, Franz Douskey, Tot Holmes, Charles Kagan, and Bill Nicholson.

In addition, we would like to thank those who provided us with needed information and material: Art Ahrens; Bill Borst, president of the St. Louis Browns Fan Club; Harrington Crissey, Jr.; Don Doxie; Ron Gabriel, president of the Brooklyn Dodgers Fan Club; Eddie Gold; Larry and Jeff Fritsch of Fritsch Cards in Stevens Point, Wisconsin; Brad Horstman; Mike Imrem; Allen Lewis; Patty McCartney; Ralph Nozaki; Gavin Riley; Joel Rippel; Bobby Risinger; Bill Sabo; Jeff Schector; Rick Westcott; Scott Winslow; and Al Yellon.

Our lineup wouldn't be such a winner without our two greatest stars, Sophie Nash and Kathy Zullo.

Contents

WELCOME TO BLOOPERSTOWN!   **xiii**

OPENING DAZE   **1**
The Most Embarrassing Moments on Opening Day

THE BOTTOM OF THE BARREL   **6**
The Worst Teams of All Time

DIAMOND DUPES   **13**
Players Who Were Bamboozled During a Game

HOLEY MITTS!   **16**
The Most Inept Fielding Performances

DOWN ON THE FAT FARM   **22**
The Most Disgracefully Out-of-Shape Heavyweights

SWAP SLOP   **26**
The Dumbest Trades Ever Made

SNOOZE PLAYS   **31**
The Most Mind-Boggling Mental Miscues

EVERY TRICK IN THE BOOK   **35**
The Sneakiest Cheating Perpetrated by Players

HITLESS WONDERS   **40**
The Most Inept Batting Performances

PARTING SHOTS   **44**
The Most Outrageous Behavior When Leaving a Game

THE REAR END OF THE FRONT OFFICE   **50**
The Most Disgraceful Actions by Owners

RUN FOR YOUR LIVES!   57
The Most Outrageous Base-Running Fiascoes

BLIND SPOTS   63
The Most Flagrantly Blown Calls by Umpires

THE ONES WHO GOT AWAY   68
Teams That Foolishly Failed to Hold on to Future Superstars

TAKE ME OUT TO THE BRAWL GAME   72
The Most Flagrant Cases of Assault and Battery on the Field

BUBBLE GUM BOZOS   80
The Most Unprofessional Baseball Cards

WELCOME TO THE BIGS!   84
The Most Inauspicious Major League Debuts

HANGING CURVES   89
The Most Pitiful Pitching Performances

THE WRECKING CREW   94
*Executives Who Wheeled and Dealed Their Team to
Rack and Ruin*

THE FALL FOLLIES   98
The Most Atrocious World Series Performances

BACKSTOP BLOCKHEADS   106
The Most Bungled Plays by Catchers

BASEBALL'S MBAs   112
Dishonorary Degrees for Managers of Blundering Actions

BOGUS BABIES   118
High-Priced Rookies Who Failed Miserably

THE MEAN TEAM   121
The Meanest Players of All Time

BOOING THE BOO BIRDS   131
The Most Unruly Behavior of Fans

HEAVE HO-HO'S   138
The Most Inglorious Ejections from a Game

RAZING THE ROOF   143
The Worst Ball Parks for Watching and Playing Games

SUBSTANDARD BEARERS   148
The Sorriest Role Models for America's Youth

PITIFUL PICKOFFS   **155**
The Most Boneheaded Pickoff Victims

TURNSTILE TURNOFFS   **159**
Ball Park Promotions That Backfired

BALLOT BOX BUNKO   **162**
The Most Unconscionable Voting for Awards and Honors

WOEFUL WINDUPS   **166**
The Most Disastrous Farewell Performances

THE ALL-TIME BASEBALL HALL OF SHAME DE-MERITORIOUS AWARD   **171**

WHO ELSE BELONGS IN THE BASEBALL HALL OF SHAME?   **174**

WELCOME TO BLOOPERSTOWN!

After our first book, *The Baseball Hall of SHAME*, was published, we soon realized that a new slate of inductees deserved to be dishonored. Our ongoing research had uncovered many more little-known ignoble incidents and hilarious happenings that warranted proper discredit. Furthermore, we had received hundreds of nominations from readers throughout the United States, Canada, and Japan. Word of our Hall even penetrated the Iron Curtain. A stalwart fan sent us his picks from Czechoslovakia.

In the spring of 1985, we visited major league cities from coast to coast, attending ball games and talking with those who make baseball America's national pastime. We were given nominations by listeners on radio call-in shows, spectators in the grandstands, sportswriters in the press boxes, and players in the clubhouses. Almost every player, manager, and coach we talked with recounted a shameful moment—sometimes involving themselves.

After sifting through all the nominations that we received or came up with through our own research, we selected those that had the best chance for enshrinement. Then we checked the accuracy of these accounts by scouring record books, archival material, and newspaper microfilm, and by conducting personal interviews. We mobilized members of the Society for American Baseball Research (of which we are members) to help us verify the facts concerning nominees. Those nominations that met our unique standards were then chosen for induction.

Just what does it mean to be in The Baseball Hall of SHAME? It's a special recognition of a moment we can all identify with—and laugh about—because each of us has at one time or another pulled a "rock."

In Chicago, WGN Radio talk-show host Roy Leonard broke the news to Lou Boudreau on the air, telling the Hall of Famer that he was now also a Hall of Shamer. Boudreau said he "felt honored." (As you may recall from our first book, Boudreau was inducted because as a rookie manager he blew a game when he blew his nose.)

Former ball player Jimmy Piersall chastised us for *not* including him in our first induction. On his radio show, he gave three reasons why he deserved Hall of Shame dishonors: He once played in a Beatles wig; he climbed the backstop during a game; and he ran the bases backward after hitting his 100th homer. Those moments failed to meet our tough standards. However, Jimmy did make it into the Hall in our second induction for a blunder described on page 13.

Many former players who had long been forgotten were delighted to hear they had been selected for induction. At least, they reasoned, they would be remembered for something—even if it was an embarrassing but funny moment.

All of the new Hall of Shamers we spoke with shared a few chuckles with us as they relived their moments of infamy. "Everybody ought to know about what happened," said the irrepressible new inductee Frenchy Bordagaray, who recounted the day he was picked off second while standing on the base. Before Lu Clinton recalled his most embarrassing moment (he literally drop-kicked a home run for the opposing team), he laughingly said, "Oh, God, I had hoped everyone forgot about that."

Unfortunately, not everyone in baseball realizes we are just having fun with the game we love so much.

In April 1985, we were thrown out of the press box in Pittsburgh during a Pirates-Mets game after a club official learned we were from The Baseball Hall of SHAME. Apparently, management was afraid that, from our press box vantage point, we would see just how shamefully the Pirates were playing.

For two years in a row, the Montreal Expos refused to give us press credentials at their spring training camp in our hometown of West Palm Beach, Florida. To the humorless team executives, there was nothing funny about our lighthearted tribute to baseball.

Perhaps no organization misunderstood our purpose more than The Baseball Hall of Fame. The powers that be banned our first book, refusing to sell it in their gift shop (which offers many other baseball books). The directors said our book is not in the best interests of the game. Fortunately, players and fans like yourself disagree.

Let the lords of baseball have their shrine in Cooperstown. We plan to erect our own shrine in "Blooperstown." We want to showcase the filed ring Whitey Ford used to cut up balls in the 1963 World Series, the two bases that Marv Throneberry missed to wipe out a clutch triple, the illegal cork-filled bat used by Graig Nettles to hit a game-winning home run, and the lineup card held by Earl Weaver when he was thrown out of a game before it even started.

We give equal recognition to the superstars and the bozos, because they have one thing in common—they all screw up at one time or another. As we say in Blooperstown, fame *and* shame are part of the game.

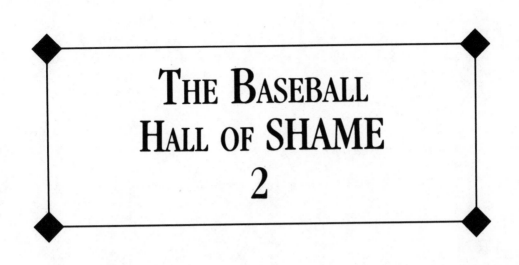

THE BASEBALL
HALL OF SHAME
2

OPENING DAZE

The Most Embarrassing Moments on Opening Day

As everyone knows, the most important day of the year is Opening Day. There is no surer sign of spring, no clearer harbinger of our recovery from cabin fever. Unfortunately, the season opener is also a red-letter day for those afflicted with a bizarre type of spring fever that has caused players, fans, and even Presidents to make complete fools of themselves. For "The Most Embarrassing Moments on Opening Day," The Baseball Hall of SHAME inducts the following:

Ebbets Field Opening Ceremonies

Brooklyn • April 9, 1913

From the day of its birth, there was little doubt that Ebbets Field would be the scene of some of the daffiest moments in baseball history.

The crowd at Opening Day ceremonies of Charles Ebbets's new playground was treated to a preview of the Flatbush Follies that would be on display there off and on for nearly half a century.

Thousands of fans started lining up at dawn to get seats. They waited and waited and waited. That's because the park superintendent had forgotten the key to the front gate. An official went back home for a spare key while the throng continued to wait.

Once the gates swung open, the fans poured into the ball park, ogling and admiring all the features. But the builder had neglected one thing—there was no press box. So the grousing sportswriters had to cover the big event from the grandstand.

Finally, the band struck up patriotic songs and the dignitaries and players started their march to center field for the flag-raising ceremony. But Charles Ebbets suddenly disrupted the procession by dropping to his knees behind second base to search in the grass for the 15 cents that he had dropped. Hot dog magnate Harry Stevens, who was walking with him, kindly offered to help Ebbets search for the coins. But Ebbets, a penny-pincher, waved him away in alarm, saying, "No, I don't want you to help me. You might find them."

Ebbets rejoined the procession as it arrived at its destination. The owner, bursting with pardonable pride, turned to an aide and said, "The flag, please."

With his face turning red, the aide replied, "Sorry, Charlie, we forgot the flag."

Franklin D. Roosevelt

President • United States of America • April 16, 1940

One of the duties Franklin D. Roosevelt enjoyed the most as President of the United States was throwing out the ceremonial first ball on Opening Day.

After eight years as Chief Executive, he had had plenty of experience doing the honors. Nevertheless, Roosevelt threw the wildest first ball in major league history.

On that fateful crisp April afternoon, the President stood up in the bunting-covered first row at Griffith Stadium in Washington, D.C. to carry on the happy springtime ritual initiated 30 years earlier by President William Howard Taft. (On Opening Day, 1910, umpire Billy Evans walked over to the President's box and, on the spur of the moment, asked Taft if he would like to toss out the first ball. He gladly accepted.)

Now it was F.D.R.'s turn. Like the five presidents before him, Roosevelt was right-handed. Like the five presidents before him, Roosevelt didn't have much of a throwing arm. Unlike the five presidents before him, Roosevelt threw a most embarrassing first ball.

As the players from the Washington Senators and Boston Red Sox gathered on the field in front of the President, F.D.R. cocked his arm and threw—and hit *Washington Post* photographer Irving Schlossenberg right in the camera!

Streakers and Strippers

Chicago • April 5, 1974

Opening Day hysteria at White Sox Park in 1974 literally peeled the inhibitions from a bunch of fans who turned the game into a carnival for streakers and strippers.

Despite frigid 35-degree weather, the naughty fans doffed their clothes and sprinted, strutted, or merely stood in the nude, freezing their fannies. There was no accurate box score of the strippers' performances since some of the frolickers were hidden from the view of the press by wide-eyed spectators who crowded in for a closer look.

One well-endowed young woman strolled topless in the upper deck. When ushers and security guards began to remove her from the premises, the fans, who didn't want her to leave, threw debris at the authorities. One vendor passed out from all the excitement and was taken away on a stretcher.

Meanwhile, a young man beneath the broadcast booth stood up and slowly disrobed to the cheers of the warmly dressed spectators. Nearby, a beefy, mustachioed man weighing about 230 pounds stripped down to his boxer shorts. An inning later, he dropped his drawers to his knees.

Then a gray-haired fellow jumped out of the left field stands and cavorted on the field in his long underwear. That inspired a young man clad only in a Sox batting helmet to vault over the box seat rail and onto the field. Free and naked, the lean streaker leaped about in an improvised ballet, an aspiring Nijinsky in the buff. His show lasted 57 seconds and ended with a dramatic headstand before he returned to his seat.

Four streakers and strippers were arrested, while several others were kicked out of the stadium. Declared Chisox manager Chuck Tanner, "If it goes beyond Opening Day, the average fan couldn't take it."

Washington Park Fans

Brooklyn • April 11, 1912

A seething mob of raucous fans who refused to leave the playing field of an overcrowded ball park turned the Opening Day game between the New York Giants and Brooklyn Dodgers into a ridiculous farce.

As fans stood along the foul lines and ringed the diamond only a few yards away from the bases, 17 routine fly balls fell into the crowd for ground-rule doubles in a travesty won by the Giants 18–3.

It seems that about 25,000 people—7,000 more than could be seated in Brooklyn's Washington Park—showed up at the game. Because management had oversold tickets, the stands and aisles were jammed. In addition, wily fans had sneaked in after busting a hole in the left field fence. Once inside, they refused to budge, defying the combined efforts of the police, team management, and even the ball players themselves to bring about law and order.

When the Dodgers ran out onto the field before the game, they couldn't practice throwing the ball because the crowd had swallowed them up. Park police tried to push the mob back. In the surge, people were stepped on, hats were smashed, and coats were torn off spectators' backs.

Players from both teams took their bats and, forming a long line, charged the crowd. But the fans fought back and refused to give up more than a few feet. The playing field could not be cleared.

Hoodlums raided the boxes and carried all the chairs vacated by disgusted occupants to the base lines and stood up on them, erecting a wall of humanity that hid the playing field from spectators in the stands. Fights broke out as angry people in the grandstand threw debris at those who blocked their view.

When Mayor William Gaynor was asked to throw out the first ball, he couldn't see the diamond, so he just tossed the ball into the crowd. Some fans were so bold they took possession of the teams' benches, forcing the players to sit on the ground.

The only people who saw the game at all were those in the top rows of the stands, the fans standing on chairs and benches along the base lines, and the policemen who stood in front of the crowd. The cops became so interested in the game after the first inning that they made no attempt to govern the mob. Meanwhile, two fans who had climbed up the wire backstop yelled down a play-by-play account to the news-hungry sportswriters who couldn't see any of the action.

New York manager John McGraw took full advantage of the ground rule adopted for the day by ordering his team to loft fly balls into the crowd whenever possible. The Giants racked up 13 cheap ground-rule doubles, while the Dodgers managed only four.

Finally, umpire Bill Klem could tolerate the debacle no longer. Although there was still plenty of light at the end of the sixth inning, Klem conveniently called the game "on account of darkness." It didn't matter. Most fans couldn't see the game anyway.

Ronald Reagan

President • United States of America • April 2, 1984

In the midst of pitching his Reaganomics to Congress in the spring of 1984, President Ronald Reagan took time out to participate in Opening Day ceremonies.

But at the ball park, he forgot some basics in supply-side economics when he tried to buy hot dogs.

About 90 minutes before game time, Reagan decided to make a surprise trip to Baltimore's Memorial Stadium for the opener between the Orioles and the Chicago White Sox.

For the ceremonial first ball, Reagan stepped onto the field and threw a low-breaking slider that Orioles catcher Rick Dempsey snagged just before it hit the ground. After leaving the field, Reagan threw an economic curveball to a hot dog vendor. The President ordered four $2 hot dogs. Then Reagan, who often notes that he has a degree in economics, tried to pay for the doggies with a $5 bill.

THE BOTTOM OF THE BARREL

The Worst Teams of All Time

Some teams belong at the top of the standings. Others belong in a Marx Brothers movie. Their pitchers have trouble finding the mound, let alone home plate. Their hitters get no-hit in batting practice. And their fielders act as if they are auditioning for a vaudeville routine. Right from Opening Day, these teams tumble directly into the cellar—and stay there. For "The Worst Teams of All Time," The Baseball Hall of SHAME inducts the following:

St. Louis Browns Franchise

1902–53

From the day they lost their very first game to the day they lost their very last game, the St. Louis Browns didn't just habitualize losing; they institutionalized it.

Simply put, the Browns were the worst franchise in major league history.

During their 52 years of existence, the Browns spent so much time in the second division it seemed as though they had signed a lease. They finished last 10 times and seventh 12 times, and in each of eight different years lost 100 or more games. Only 12 times did they manage to reach the first division. St. Louis compiled a sorry all-time won-loss record of 3,414–4,465, for a miserable .433 percentage, the lowest of any franchise in the annals of baseball.

Donning the Browns' insipid uniforms were a woebegone collection of misfits—including a midget, a one-armed outfielder, a hypnotist, and a broadcaster. The team couldn't possibly win any respect, not with names like Baby Doll Jacobson, Clyde Kluttz, Grover Lowdermilk, Hill Billy Bildilli, Bingo Binks, Stinky Davis, Inky Strange, and, of course, Vitautis Casimirus Tamulis.

While other teams won and made it look easy, the Browns lost and made it look difficult. It was their tradition. Somehow it seems fitting that they made a promotional appearance for a Wall Street brokerage house in 1929—and weeks later the stock market collapsed.

The Browns mirrored the malaise that plagued the country by failing to have a single winning season in the 1930s. Fans found the team as exciting as a soup kitchen line. For one game in 1933, only 34 spectators bothered to show up. The major league attendance record for a regular season game is 84,587 (in Cleveland); the Browns failed to draw that many at home for their *entire season* in 1935.

The years from 1937–39, in which St. Louis dropped, squandered away, and booted 316 games, included the club record year (1939), when the team lost 111 games and won only 18 home games. The players just went through the motions. Recalled infielder Mark Christman, "You would try to get yourself up. But when you know you're going to be eight runs behind after the first couple of innings, there's just no way you could pull yourself up to really go out there and bear down one hundred percent."

The awful team entered the 1940s bereft of any talent, money, fans, or hope. When Luke Sewell was named the new manager in 1941, he received as many condolences as congratulations.

The roster was filled with aged and ailing journeymen who had failed to qualify for military service. The Browns were so bad that even the wartime Army didn't want them. Although 340 ball players were in the military service by 1944, not a single member of the Browns was inducted during the 1943–44 off-season. St. Louis started the 1944 season with 18 4-Fs on its roster.

Nothing short of a world war could have made the Browns a contender. Among the 16 major league teams in existence at the time, only the Browns had never won a pennant. Yet somehow, in that talent-bare season of 1944, this ragtag team finished first for the one and only time. Then it lost the World Series to the crosstown rival Cardinals in six games.

To show how much Browns management thought of the team, one-armed outfielder Pete Gray was signed to "strengthen" the club. Although admired for his courage, he was of little help. Gray played in 77 games and batted a lowly .218 in his only year in the bigs.

In 1946, the Browns tumbled to seventh, and remained stuck in the second division until their demise in 1953. Radio broadcaster Dizzy Dean was so upset by the Browns' ineptness in 1947 that he announced on the air that he could do better. St. Louis management took him up on his boast. Even though Dean hadn't pitched in six years, he hurled 3 2/3 innings of shutout ball and laced a base hit in his only time at bat.

In 1950, the team was in desperate need of help. But rather than find a solution through trades or promotion of minor leaguers, the Browns turned to David Tracy, a psychologist, who was hired to hypnotize the team into winners. After a few sessions, Tracy announced that the Browns were suffering from "loser's syndrome." Being traded to the Browns was the psychological equivalent of being shipped to Siberia, he said, adding that new players arrived in a dejected frame of mind. Fans and players, none of whom had psychology degrees, already knew this. Like most everything else the Browns tried, Tracy's hypnosis didn't improve the team. The "whammy man," as the press labeled him, was summarily dismissed.

In 1951, new owner Bill Veeck tried to inject some life into the team. He gave them a fatal dose of folly instead. Veeck conjured up crazy promotional stunts, such as letting the fans call plays while manager Zack Taylor sat in a rocking chair atop the St. Louis dugout. On August 24, 1,115 "grandstand managers" sat behind the dugout and decided strategy by flashing "Yes" or "No" cards after coaches posed questions at key junctures. The majority ruled—and managed the Browns to a 5–3 win over the Philadelphia Athletics.

But Veeck's wildest brainstorm was sending 3-foot, 7-inch midget Eddie Gaedel up to the plate to pinch-hit against the stunned Detroit Tigers on August 19. On Veeck's orders, Gaedel, wearing number 1/8, crouched low and didn't dare swing. He believed the owner's threat that a rifleman on the roof had orders to shoot the little Brownie if he so much as started to swing. As expected, Gaedel walked. He was removed for a pinch runner and never played again. His time at bat made the Browns seem even more ridiculous than they were.

In their final season, in 1953, the Browns sank to depths previously reached only by U-boats. The team attracted more flies than fans as attendance dwindled to an appalling average of less than 4,000 a game.

Bill Veeck was broke, and he sold players to meet payrolls. When Bobo Holloman tossed a no-hitter in his first start on May 6, Veeck had to borrow money from a friend to reward the pitcher.

The franchise's last gasp, it's final game ever, was like a capsule of its half century of trials and tribulations.

Wanting one last masochistic look at their dying team, a crowd of 3,174 showed up at Sportsman's Park to watch the last-place Browns tangle with the Chicago White Sox.

The Browns fan club from Chicago journeyed to St. Louis and held a mock funeral for the team outside the gates. Browns fans in the right field pavilion showed their feelings in a more hostile manner. They hanged Veeck in effigy, then, in the fifth inning, tossed the dummy onto the field.

So desperate was the Browns' financial situation that they almost ran out of baseballs for the game. Because they had only two dozen on hand, the Browns took neither batting nor fielding practice. The umpires, aware of the situation, allowed baseballs to remain in play that ordinarily would have been tossed out.

The situation was exacerbated when the game went into extra innings. Fans were asked to throw foul balls hit into the stands back onto the field.

Some did. Some didn't. Finally, the White Sox loaned the Browns some scarred, defaced practice balls with which to finish the game.

The White Sox won, 2–1. It was the Brown's 100th defeat—and mercifully, its last.

By the end of 1953, the American League had forced Veeck to sell out to a Baltimore syndicate, bringing the curtain down on the comic tragedy that was the St. Louis Browns.

No longer would the citizens of St. Louis, proud of their city's shoe factories and breweries, utter the sardonic slogan that had put the Browns in civic perspective: "First in shoes, first in booze, and last in the American League."

Pittsburgh Pirates

1952

Pittsburgh Pirates general manager Branch Rickey decided to build a pennant-winning team with youth. So he launched "Operation Peach Fuzz." It turned into "Mission Impossible."

After dishing out about a half million dollars in bonuses to teenagers fresh off the sandlots, Rickey fielded a wet-behind-the-ears team that played some of the most shameful baseball ever seen at major league prices.

The "Rickey Dinks," as they were appropriately nicknamed, won only 42 games, lost a whopping 112, and finished last, 54 1/2 games out of first.

Raising the eyebrows and ire of fans, Rickey stocked the roster with 17 untried youngsters, all of whom were playing in the bigs for the very first time. It would prove to be the *only* year for eight of them.

Among the 19-year-olds upon whom Rickey counted were first baseman Tom Bartirome and outfielders Bobby Del Greco and Lee Walls. They batted .220, .217, and .118 respectively. The Pirates had so many baby-faced hurlers the bull pen looked like a playpen. The kiddie corps included 18-year-old Jim Waugh, 1–6, 6.36 ERA; 19-year-old Ron Kline, 0–7, 5.49 ERA; 18-year-old Bill "Ding Dong" Bell, 0–1, 4.60 ERA; and the infamous Ron Necciai. The 19-year-old right-hander was plucked from Class D ball by Rickey, who swore the kid was the next Dizzy Dean. The only similarity between the two pitchers was that they both wore baseball uniforms. After recording a dreadful 1–6 mark and a 7.08 ERA, Necciai never pitched in the majors again.

The "Rickey Dinks" got off to a slow start, losing 10 of their first 14 games. Then they fell into a slump that lasted all season. Their best month was August, when they were rained out of five games.

The team was so bad that back-to-back homers meant a four-bagger by

Ralph Kiner one day and another round-tripper by him the next game. Pittsburgh measured victory in terms of defeat. A 5–4 loss was a good day. A big rally was veteran Joe Garagiola hitting a windblown double. The Pirates talked a much better game than they played, spurring Cincinnati Reds manager Rogers Hornsby to tell them, "You guys have a fifty-fifty team. You get 'em out in the clubhouse but lose on the field."

Beleaguered manager Billy Meyer needed the patience of a kindergarten teacher. Once, when rookie Dick Hall was on first, Meyer flashed him the steal sign. But Hall didn't move. After the next pitch, Meyer repeated the sign. Again, Hall stayed put. Meyer gave the sign a third time. Still, Hall didn't budge. At the end of the inning, Meyer confronted Hall and said, "I gave you the steal sign three times. Why didn't you run?" Hall answered, "I didn't think you meant it."

Hall learned how to alibi from veteran Catfish Metkovich, who was a master at making up excuses. Once, when he pinch-hit against Boston Braves pitcher Max Surkont, Metkovich took three straight called strikes. When he returned to the dugout, he told his teammates that he hadn't stood a chance against Surkont because the hurler "threw me that radio ball—you can hear it, but you can't see it."

Metkovich symbolized the Pirates' futility in a game against the Brooklyn Dodgers. Line drives flew past his head and through his legs all day at first base. When a hard grounder ricocheted off his shins for a single, an exasperated Metkovich turned to umpire Augie Donatelli and shouted, "For Cripes sakes, Augie, don't just stand there. Get a glove and help me out!"

The Pirates triggered further laughter when they sported batting helmets for the first time. The players were called everything from coal miners to space cadets. Opposing pitchers wondered why a last place team needed the protective hats. After all, said one hurler, "Who's going to throw at .200 hitters?"

When one Pirate rookie asked if the hats would be better if they had some foam rubber in them, veteran Clyde McCullough replied, "No, I think they'd be better if we had some ball players in them."

Boston Braves

1935

If any baseball club deserved to be labeled "America's team" in 1935, it was the Boston Braves. They represented the single most important issue of the day—the Depression.

The hapless Braves lost unceasingly, capriciously, and dispiritedly—in perfect harmony with the hopelessness of their times. They wound up with the worst record in the National League in this century with a woeful mark of 38–115 and a horrendous winning percentage of only .248. The Braves tumbled so far behind into last place, 61 1/2 games out, that they needed a telescope to see the seventh-place Phillies 26 games ahead of them.

They lost in close games and in routs. They lost on dropped pop flies and muffed grounders. They even lost to the Arthur Fisher Shoe Co. team of Randolph, Massachusetts, in an exhibition game.

Part of the problem was that the Braves needed three kinds of pitching—left-handed, right-handed, and relief. Ben Cantwell dropped 13 decisions in a row on his way to an awful mark of 4–25. Hardly intimidating, Cantwell struck out only 34 batters in 210 innings. Manager Bill McKechnie's wisdom in sending Cantwell to the mound so often can be questioned. Cantwell's courage in going to the mound can not. The other starters were nearly as crummy: Earl Brandt, 5–19; Bob Smith, 8–18; and the "ace" of the staff, Fred Frankhouse, 11–15.

Another problem for the Braves was the aging Babe Ruth. He joined Boston after the Yankees released him at the end of the 1934 season. Judge Emil Fuchs, owner of the financially-strapped Braves, signed Ruth as a gate attraction. But at age 40—his body bloated and out of shape from years of fast living—Ruth hurt the team more than he helped it. His new teammates resented him because he drew a large salary, flouted training rules, lived apart from the rest of the players when on the road, and showed a definite lack of interest in the team's welfare. All of this could have been tolerated had he produced at the plate. But he hit only 6 homers and batted a paltry .181 in 28 games before quitting baseball for good, two months into the season.

Boston had just one bona fide star, Wally Berger, who walloped 34 homers and drove in 130 RBIs. Without him, the Braves would have finished last in the lowly Sally League.

Figuring they were suffering enough out in the real world, fans stayed away from Braves Field. Fewer than 100 rooters were on hand for a July 28 doubleheader in which Boston lost both ends to Brooklyn. "There didn't seem to be an atom of fight in the Braves' makeup," reported one newspaper. Three days later the Braves game was postponed so that their ball park could be used for the Danno O'Mahoney-Don George wrestling match.

Because the team was close to bankruptcy, the players spent their scheduled off-days playing exhibition games against semi-pros and minor leaguers. It was believed that the Braves were more likely to draw paying crowds the further away from Boston they played.

Against National League teams, the Braves averaged just one win for every three losses. They hit a 15-game losing skid in July and, when they finally won, a local headline read, "The Slaughter of the Innocents Is Halted."

But the Braves went right back to their winless ways. From August 18 until September 14, the lackluster team won only two of 30 games.

When the embarrassing season finally came to an end, new club management wanted to remove the stigma of utter failure from the team. So the club invited fans to submit a new name for the Braves.

Thousands of names, from Sacred Cods to Bankrupts, were submitted. The judges picked the short-lived moniker Bees. Braves or Bees, the team still was a second division loser the following year. To paraphrase Shakespeare, "What's in a name? That which we call the Braves by any other name would lose as badly."

DIAMOND DUPES

Players Who Were Bamboozled During a Game

Many ball players are con men at heart, often making sneaky attempts to trick an opponent into screwing up a play. The perpetrators usually fail because the opposing players are just as cunning as they are. Every once in a while, however, a sucker comes along who swallows the bait—hook, line, and sinker. It's then that the hoodwinked chump learns just how far it is to the dugout. For "Players Who Were Bamboozled During a Game," The Baseball Hall of SHAME inducts the following:

Jimmy Piersall

Outfielder • Boston, A.L. • Aug. 4, 1953

During his eight years with the Boston Red Sox, Jimmy Piersall liked to be called the "Waterbury Wizard." But he didn't look too wizardly after being victimized by a classic ruse.

In the seventh inning of a game against the visiting St. Louis Browns, Piersall was on second base representing the tying run. After center fielder Johnny Groth caught a fly ball for the second out, he threw to shortstop Billy Hunter, who then walked to the mound to talk with pitcher Duane Pillette.

Hunter pretended to give the hurler the ball, but in actuality, the crafty infielder concealed it in his glove. As Hunter walked back to his position, he quietly alerted umpire Bill Summers to be ready for a trick play.

Hunter then ambled over to his easy mark and struck up a friendly chat with the unsuspecting Piersall. "Hey, Jim, there's dirt all over that bag," said Hunter. "Why don't you kick it and get the dirt off."

Like a trusting soul, Piersall obligingly stepped off the base to give it a boot. Before Jimmy had a chance to move another muscle, Hunter quickly tagged him, and Summers called him out. Red-faced, Piersall didn't say a word. He just glared at the smirking Hunter.

But Piersall got the last laugh moments later. In the top of the eighth, Hunter led off with a single and was sacrificed to second. Given the steal sign, he took a big lead—and was promptly picked off.

Johnny Bench

Catcher • Cincinnati, N.L. • Oct. 18, 1972

Johnny Bench, who played in 23 World Series games, was often an October hero. But in the third game of the 1972 Series, Bench looked more like an April fool.

The Cincinnati Reds star was at bat with runners on second and third, one out, and his team ahead 1–0 in the eighth inning. After Bench ran the count to 3-and-2, Oakland A's manager Dick Williams went to the mound to talk with pitcher Rollie Fingers and catcher Gene Tenace.

It was a crucial moment in the tight game. Bench figured the A's were discussing whether to pitch to him or walk him intentionally. When play resumed, he thought he knew what they had decided.

Standing behind and to the right of the plate, Tenace pointed to first base and extended his gloved hand, the traditional gesture for an intentional base on balls. Bench relaxed and waited for the wide pitch he expected.

As Fingers threw, Tenace suddenly crouched behind the plate. The ball caught the outside corner. To his utter distress, Johnny Bench, a thinking man's ball player, realized he had been suckered into a called third strike. Casting his eyes to the ground, Bench shuffled back to the dugout, a victim of a baseball con job.

Told that Fingers said the pitch was one of the best he had thrown all year, Bench replied, "Why me? He does it when 50 million people are watching."

Leon Wagner

Outfielder • San Francisco, N.L. • July 1, 1958

If gypsies had known how easy it was to hornswoggle Leon Wagner, they would have dropped their nomadic ways and camped out at his doorstep. He showed his gullibility when he fell for a simple hoax during a game.

Wagner, then a San Francisco Giants rookie, was playing left field against the Chicago Cubs in Wrigley Field when batter Tony Taylor lashed a first-inning shot over third base. The ball landed fair and then bounded toward the Chicago bull pen, located in foul territory along the left field line. The hit seemed like nothing more than a typical double.

But then the Cubs in the bull pen led Wagner astray. They leaped off the bench and peered under it as if they were looking for the ball. Their actions convinced Wagner to start a frantic search over, under, and around the bench. But he couldn't find the ball because the flim-flammers had given him a bum steer. The ball was resting on a rain gutter 20 feet past the bull pen.

By the time Wagner realized he had been duped, Taylor had already dashed around the bases for an inside-the-park home run.

HOLEY MITTS!

The Most Inept Fielding Performances

You can tell who they are in the box score by their first initial, E. They are the fabulous fumblers who somehow make it to the bigs with holes in their gloves. These players catch hell from fans more often than they catch balls. They boot so many balls they belong on a soccer field, not a baseball diamond. For "The Most Inept Fielding Performances," The Baseball Hall of SHAME inducts the following:

Zeke "Bananas" Bonura

First baseman • Chicago-Washington, A.L.; New York-Chicago, N.L. • 1934–40

Zeke Bonura was nicknamed "Bananas" for good reason.

He *was* bananas.

Although certifiably the worst-fielding first baseman of his time, the colorful big lug made few errors—because he cheerfully waved good-bye to outfield-bound grounders that he could easily have caught. Bonura simply never moved off a dime. He drove his managers crazy by giving the Fascist salute to bouncing balls that were no more than five feet away from him.

After watching Bonura bid farewell to yet another easy grounder, Washington Senators owner Calvin Griffith sputtered in anger, "Bonura is a no-account. In more than 50 years in baseball, he's the worst and most overpaid big league ball player I've ever seen!"

Bonura hit well enough to stay in the majors for seven years, despite fielding that was less than perfect and more than frightful. Though he went through the motions with lusty zeal and boisterous enthusiasm, fielding just didn't seem all that important to the 6-foot, 210-pound first baseman.

Bonura had such an easy-going nature that he was always willing to listen to yarns from enemy first base coaches during games. He was being friendly. They were being devious. They deliberately took his mind off the game, making it easier for a hitter to bounce a batted ball past him.

Every once in a while, Bonura flashed his temper and consequently lost track of the game. On April 24, 1938, the Senators were beating the Yankees 3–2 in the eighth inning, but New York, with one out, had loaded the bases.

On a potential double-play ball, the Senators got the runner out at second but the batter beat the throw to first as the tying run scored. Bonura, playing first for Washington, whirled around to argue with umpire Johnny Quinn, forgetting that the ball he held in his glove was still in play. As Bonura continued to rant and rave, Yankee runner Joe Gordon, who had gone from second to third on the groundout, raced around third and slid across the plate with the winning run.

Bonura turned first base into a shambles when he played for the Chicago White Sox. To make sure that balls hit directly at him would not slip by, he used an unorthodox feet-together fielding stance that made him look like an overstuffed praying mantis. He considered it something of a moral victory whenever he kept a grounder from getting past him.

The patience of Chicago manager Jimmy Dykes wore thin by 1937, especially after Bonura, in a tight game against the Tigers, let a ball get by him for the game-winning hit.

"Could Bonura have gotten that ball?" Dykes asked White Sox catcher Luke Sewell.

"No," replied Sewell.

"Why not? It was hit right at him. What are you trying to do, cover for him?"

"I merely said Bonura couldn't have gotten it. If you want to ask me about the seven other first basemen in the league, well, that's something else."

Al Selbach

Outfielder • Washington-Cincinnati-New York, N.L.;
Baltimore-Washington-Boston, A.L. • 1894–1906

Fans thought the way Al Selbach played the outfield was a joke. But he was dead serious the whole time.

More often than not, Selbach looked like a recruit for the Keystone Cops, displaying such unintended fielding zaniness that his own glove was embarrassed. There was no one quite like him—the record book attests to that. Selbach is the only player in major league history to have two shameful records—for the most outfield errors both in an inning and in a game.

He first bumbled his way into the annals of baseball as a Baltimore Oriole when he committed *five* errors in one game. He was impersonating a left fielder in a contest against the St. Louis Browns on August 19, 1902. Three times an easy fly ball fell into his glove and three times it bounced out and plopped onto the ground. Two times a routine single headed straight toward him and two times it rolled right between his legs.

Selbach's fielding became such a travesty that the Baltimore fans cheered derisively and shouted bawdy advice whenever a ball was hit to left field. There wasn't much else they could do as his botchery handed the opposing Browns an 11–4 victory.

In the next year and a half, Selbach unintentionally brought hilarity to the outfield as a member of the Washington Senators. Having established his ignominious fielding record in Baltimore, he went after another new mark in Washington—and got it.

It came on June 23, 1904, in the top of the eighth inning in a 2–2 game against the New York Yankees. New York had a runner on first when a single was hit to left field. Selbach scooped up the ball and heaved it so wildly over the third baseman's head that both hitter and runner scored. A few batters later, Selbach misplayed another single, putting a runner on second and allowing a third runner to score. Now he was on a roll, and, perhaps sensing immortality, he seized the moment to drop a routine fly ball for two more runs. All told, Selbach's record-tying three outfield errors in one inning gave the Yankees five unearned runs in the frame, enough for a 7–4 New York win.

The Senators were not amused. Just days after Selbach's fielding debacle, they dumped him.

Stan Musial

Outfielder • St. Louis, N.L. • May 14, 1944

Stan Musial suffered his most mortifying fielding moment on a heads-up play.

Stan the Man was playing center field for the St. Louis Cardinals in a game against the visiting Philadelphia Phillies. At age 24, Musial was already a star, both with his glove and with his bat. But on this day, he was upstaged by 40-year-old teammate Pepper Martin. Although it was Martin's final year in the bigs, the old "Wild Horse of the Osage" fielded his position in right field like a frisky colt, dashing back and forth to make one sensational catch after another.

Because few balls were hit to center during most of the game, Musial didn't have an opportunity to wow the fans. But in the eighth inning, when the Phillies posed their only threat of the day, Musial finally had the fans buzzing.

With two runners on, Philly batter Jimmy Wasdell lofted a towering fly to center. Musial glided back and effortlessly waited for the ball to land in his glove. Instead, the ball landed smack dab on his head and knocked him down! Poor Stan had lost the ball in the sun.

Pepper Martin retrieved the ball and fired it to the infield, holding Wasdell to a run-scoring single. Then Martin rushed to Musial's side.

"Are you hurt, kid?" Martin asked.

Musial rubbed his aching head and mumbled, "No."

"Then you don't mind if I laugh, do you?" Without waiting for an answer, Martin doubled over and laughed himself limp, holding up the game until he regained his composure. On the very next play, Martin made a spectacular catch, robbing Tony Lupien of a triple and saving the game.

Martin grabbed the headlines. Musial grabbed the aspirin.

Lu Clinton

Outfielder • Boston, A.L. • Aug. 9, 1960

In his rookie year with the Boston Red Sox, outfielder Lu Clinton once played as if he were a football player—and drop-kicked a home run for the Cleveland Indians.

The game was tied 3–3 in the bottom of the fifth inning when Cleveland first baseman Vic Power stepped to the plate with a runner aboard and two out. He slammed a high drive over the head of Clinton in right field. The ball hit the top of the wire fence and bounced back toward Clinton, who was running with his back to the infield.

Before the outfielder could react to the carom, the ball fell in front of him. But it never touched the ground. The ball hit the foot of the still-running Clinton—who then proceeded to accidently kick it right over the fence! Because the ball never touched the ground, umpire Hal Smith ruled the hit a home run—one that proved to be the game-winner.

"Our pitcher that day was Bill Monbouquette," recalled Clinton. "He didn't say a whole lot after the game. He didn't have to. I knew he was really hacked off at me."

Tommy Glaviano

Third baseman • St. Louis, N.L. • May 18, 1950

No infielder ever blew a game more shamefully than did Tommy Glaviano.

The St. Louis Cardinals third baseman played the ninth inning against the Brooklyn Dodgers as if he were in a Bums uniform.

The Cards entered the final frame at Ebbets Field with an 8–4 lead, but the Dodgers rallied, and with one out and a run in, loaded the bases. Then Brooklyn discovered the secret to victory—hit the ball to Glaviano.

Roy Campanella slapped a grounder to Glaviano, but the third sacker threw wide to second base trying for a force-out. The bases remained loaded as another run crossed the plate, making the score 8-6. The next batter, Eddie Miksis, hit another grounder to Glaviano. Once again, the infielder threw wide, this time to home, allowing the Dodgers' seventh run to score. Up stepped Pee Wee Reese, who couldn't wait to rap a ball to third. Sure enough, Reese sent a grounder to Glaviano. The ball rolled between his legs as the tying and winning runs crossed the plate.

Glaviano's three consecutive ninth-inning errors gifted Brooklyn with four runs for a shocking 9–8 victory.

For most people, three's a charm. For Tommy Glaviano, three was a curse.

Down on the Fat Farm

The Most Disgracefully Out-of-Shape Heavyweights

Much of baseball tradition is written in food stains by players who fight the battle of the bulge—and lose. These porkers handle a knife and fork with more skill than a bat and ball. Whenever they step foot on the diamond, there's always the danger it might break off beneath their weight and become its own continent. For "The Most Disgracefully Out-of-Shape Heavyweights," The Baseball Hall of SHAME inducts the following:

Cy Rigler

Umpire • 1906–35

To 6-foot, 240-pound ump Cy Rigler, home plate was something you ate off of. He was notorious for delaying the start of second games of doubleheaders so he could enjoy a leisurely and large lunch.

The vendors loved Cy. After the first game, he would stroll over to the grandstand and gorge himself, stretching intermission to as long as 40 minutes.

Once, after a game in Cincinnati, the champion trencherman consumed five pigs knuckles, five orders of sauerkraut, five boiled potatoes, five ears of corn, three limburger sandwiches, five bottles of beer, and three cups of coffee. Recalled the concessionaire, Hal "Hot Dog" Stevens: "As he was leaving, Cy turned to me and said, 'Hal, thanks for the snack.' "

On another day at Ebbets Field, the doubleheader intermission lasted longer than usual. The press box scribes rigged up a phony telegram that was delivered to Cy as he came out for the second game. The wire read: "Hereafter confine yourself to three courses and get the second game started sooner. John A. Heydler, president, National League."

Rigler shoved the telegram into his back pocket and never gave it another thought. He continued to pig out on double helpings during doubleheaders.

Bob "Fats" Fothergill

Outfielder • Detroit-Chicago-Boston, A.L. • 1922–33

Roly-poly Fats Fothergill looked like a toadstool with a glandular problem.

The 5-foot, 10-inch, 230-pound outfielder loved to eat. Spotting Fothergill with a big bundle under his arm in the clubhouse one day in 1927, Tigers manager George Moriarty asked him if he was carrying his laundry. "Laundry, nothing," said Fats. "It's my lunch."

When he reported to spring training in 1928, Fats was so overweight he went on a crash reducing program. He exercised for hours in a rubber suit, took Turkish baths, and followed a strict diet. It was too much for him. During the first month of the season, he was so weak he couldn't hit the ball and fell into a horrible batting slump.

He also grew increasingly testier, until he finally cracked in a tight ball game when umpire Bill Dinneen called him out on a third strike. Uncharacteristically enraged, Fothergill seized Dinneen and bit him on the arm. For this shocking display of cannibalism, Fats was tossed out of the game. "It's okay by me," Fats muttered to the ump. "That's the first bite of meat I've had in a month."

George Brace Photo

23

Shanty Hogan

Catcher • Boston-New York, N.L.; Washington, A.L. • 1925–37

At 6-foot, 1-inch and 260 pounds, Shanty Hogan achieved the major league distinction as "the biggest catcher in captivity."

He was so fat that when he led off the inning with a walk, he filled the bases. He stretched triples into singles.

He didn't run around the bases, he waddled. In a game against the New York Giants in 1935, Hogan chugged toward second base after his Boston Braves teammate Huck Betts hit the ball past the first baseman for what should have been a single. However, right fielder Mel Ott scooped up the ball and threw the lead-footed Hogan out at second.

When he was traded to the Giants, Shanty's enormous appetite caused manager John McGraw nothing but heartburn. McGraw fined Hogan so many times that the catcher lamented to reporters, "Mr. McGraw lives in a magnificent mansion and I paid for every stick of wood in it."

Shanty's weight upset the manager from the very first day the catcher reported to spring training in 1928. McGraw took one look at Mr. Whopper and left orders with the hotel waiters that Shanty wasn't allowed to even look at cakes and pies. Instead of losing weight, Shanty added several pounds. An investigation by the Giants revealed a conspiracy. Through a clever arrangement, a friendly waiter would bring Shanty a half of pie whenever he ordered "spinach." When McGraw found out, he parked trainer Doc Knowles at Shanty's elbow for every meal. "That guy gets between me and the soup," the rotund catcher moaned.

Before spring training in 1932, Hogan had his picture taken working out in a rowing machine to convince McGraw that he was trying to keep fit. McGraw was very suspicious. The photograph showed Hogan rowing in patent leather shoes.

Early in the 1932 season, McGraw told Hogan that unless he dropped 30 pounds to a weight of 228, he wouldn't play. "I can't go hungry," wailed Hogan. "A big man like me can't live on orange juice and a promise." He patted his big belly and added, "This is quite a carcass." It sure was.

Jumbo Brown

Pitcher • Chicago-Cincinnati-New York, N.L.; New York, A.L. • 1925–41

At 295 pounds, Jumbo Brown was undoubtedly the heaviest major leaguer to play regularly in this century. He was a so-so pitcher who threw fastballs, curveballs, and the biggest shadow in baseball.

Seeing Jumbo for the first time, New York sportswriter Frank Graham wrote: "He weighs two pounds more than an elephant, but that's an exaggeration—by two pounds, anyway."

The tonnage was standard equipment for Brown ever since the end of the 1927 season, when he had his tonsils removed. His weight ballooned from 197 pounds to a whopping 265 pounds by the time he reported to spring training a few months later. Cleveland Indians general manager Billy Evans didn't want to carry a human blimp on the team, so he shipped Brown to the minors.

Three years later, the Yankees invited Brown to their spring training camp. Jumbo had to work out in his undershirt because the team didn't have a uniform big enough to fit him. His weight made headlines on March 3, 1933, when he inveigled the Yankees into a game of leapfrog. As he leaped over his teammates, they collapsed one by one. After the human wreckage had been cleared away, the Yankees were dismayed to learn that outfielder Sam Byrd and catcher Cy Perkins were injured.

Nevertheless, the Yankees kept Jumbo on their roster and billed him as "the man who swallowed a taxi cab." Naturally, for a player that fat, pitching during the dog days of summer was rough. In a game on June 10, 1933, he took himself out because he was too tired and woozy—"which was just as well for all concerned," read a newspaper account of the game. "For one thing, carrying him out would have taxed the strength of all the other Yankees put together."

Swap Slop

The Dumbest Trades Ever Made

General managers claim they make trades to better the team. But it's often the other team they make better. Baseball is blighted with execs who couldn't recognize talent at the All-Star Game. With their skills at dealing, these GMs would trade their new Cadillac for a rusty Volkswagen and an Edsel to be named later. For "The Dumbest Trades Ever Made," The Baseball Hall of SHAME inducts the following:

Grover Cleveland Alexander for Pickles Dillhoefer and Mike Prendergast

Dec. 11, 1917

This was such a great giveaway that the Phillies should have been running a discount store.

The Phillies handed over to the Cubs 30-game winner Grover Cleveland Alexander and his catcher Bill Killefer for Mike Prendergast (9–17), his catcher Pickles Dillhoefer, and $55,000.

Philadelphia fans were understandably outraged. In eight seasons with the Phils, the future Hall of Famer had compiled a sensational 190–88 record. In his last year in Philadelphia, he won 30, lost 13, had an ERA of 1.86, completed 35 games, and recorded 8 shutouts. But with callous disregard for the fans and his team, president William Baker shipped his greatest star to the Cubs. In slightly more than eight years in Chicago, Alexander compiled a sterling 128–83 record, including 27 victories in 1920.

The cash the Phillies received in the transaction lasted longer than the two ex-Cubs. After a two-year record of 13–15, Prendergast was dumped. Pickles immediately went sour. He had more "L's" in his last name than he had hits, and by the end of the year the Phils canned Pickles.

Hal McRae for Richie Scheinblum
and Roger Nelson

Nov. 30, 1972

Cincinnati fans should have complained to the Better Business Bureau. Their team fell victim to a two-for-one deal that seemed too good to be true. It was.

The Reds traded outfielder Hal McRae to Kansas City in exchange for outfielder Richie Scheinblum and pitcher Roger Nelson.

After the deal, McRae established himself as the premier designated hitter, batting .297 or better in eight seasons and leading the Royals to six division titles. A three-time All-Star, McRae set a League Championship Series record for most runs scored.

Meanwhile, Nelson compiled a ho-hum 7–6 record before dropping out of sight. Scheinblum played only 29 games for Cincy and hit an embarrassing .222. However, he did distinguish himself in Cincinnati.

The balding 30-year-old got a special deal on a hair-weaving procedure because he agreed to pose in print advertisements for the company. In the ad, he held a can of hair spray and said, "Thanks to Hair Replacement Centers, I'm now available for hair spray commercials." Not surprisingly, no one cared.

Curt Flood for Marty Kutyna, Willard Schmidt,
and Ted Wieand

Dec. 5, 1957

It was your typical flea market swap. One sharp trader unloads his junk on a rube in exchange for a real plum.

The Cincinnati Reds were in need of pitching so they were more than willing to give up teenage infielder Curt Flood and bit player Joe Taylor for three nondescript St. Louis Cardinal pitchers.

The trio didn't solve the Reds' pitching woes. They merely prolonged it. Marty Kutyna didn't even make the team. Ted Wieand had an 0–1 record and was soon dropped, while Willard Schmidt pitched two years and finished his lackluster career at 6–7.

Meanwhile, Flood blossomed into an All-Star outfielder for the Cardinals. During his 12-year stint in St. Louis, he batted over .300 in seven seasons, led the league in hits in 1964, and spurred the Cardinals to three World Series.

Radio Announcer Lou Boudreau for Manager Charlie Grimm

May 4, 1960

With the Cubs in last place, owner Philip K. Wrigley decided to shake things up by engineering a big trade. But since he usually ended up on the short end of deals with other teams, he took his business elsewhere—to a radio station.

To the bewilderment of baseball, Wrigley cut a deal with WGN Radio, the Cubs flagship station, and sent manager Charlie Grimm to the broadcast booth in return for announcer Lou Boudreau.

It was an even trade—both sides lost.

In Boudreau's first game as manager, the Cubs held a comfortable 7–2 sixth-inning lead over the Pirates, only to lose 9–7. Things got worse for Boudreau. He tried every imaginable combination to put together a winning lineup, but nothing worked. The Cubs finished with an awful 60-94 record, equaling their worst year ever.

Meanwhile, "Jolly Cholly" Grimm did game commentary that was as colorful and sharp as an old Philco TV set.

Wrigley decided another shake-up was in order. In a bizarre move, the owner eliminated managers altogether and instituted his infamous College of Coaches—but not before trading Boudreau back to WGN for Grimm, who became one of the team's eight revolving coaches.

Graig Nettles for Charlie Spikes, John Ellis, Rusty Torres, and Jerry Kenney

Nov. 27, 1972

In 1626, the Yankees fleeced the Indians by purchasing Manhattan Island for $24 in trinkets. In baseball, 346 years later, the Yankees stuck it to the Indians once again.

The prime find this time was 28-year-old third baseman Graig Nettles. In New York, his dazzling fielding around the hot corner earned him five All-Star selections. He averaged 23 homers a season during his 11-year stay in New York and led his team to four league championships. He established the American League record for third basemen for most homers in a career and most assists in a season.

The Indians, like their 17th century counterparts, were left holding a relatively worthless bag. For Cleveland, Charlie Spikes played five so-so years as an outfielder, utility man John Ellis lasted three years, outfielder Rusty Torres played two years, and second baseman Jerry Kenney was lopped off the roster after appearing in only five games. The combined years of service in Cleveland for the futile foursome didn't equal the time Nettles served as a Yankee.

Tris Speaker for Sad Sam Jones and Fred Thomas

April 12, 1916

Future Hall of Fame outfielder Tris Speaker terrorized pitchers by hitting over .300 for seven straight years for the Boston Red Sox. So what did management do? They traded him to the Cleveland Indians for a losing pitcher, a warm body, and $55,000 in cash.

In his first year as an Indian, the "Grey Eagle" led the league with a lofty .386 batting average. For 10 of the 11 years he was with Cleveland, Speaker hit .304 or better, lifting the Indians from near the bottom of the league to seven straight first division finishes, including a World Series championship in 1920.

The Red Sox should have known better than to trade for a pitcher named Sad Sam. He lost 20 games for them in 1919. As for Thomas, he just took up space on the bench.

Sparky Lyle for Danny Cater

March 22, 1972

Dick O'Connell, the Boston Red Sox general manager, confessed, "It was the worst trade I ever made." Even doubting Thomas would agree.

Boston needed a first baseman, so it set its sights on 31-year-old Yankee infielder Danny Cater. O'Connell apparently figured that since Cater had been with five different teams in eight years, he must be good, or else why would everyone be trading for him? The Yankees knew the truth: everyone was unloading him.

Now it was New York's turn to cast Cater off. The team traded him to Boston straight up for Sparky Lyle, the Red Sox top relief specialist.

In his first year in pinstripes, Lyle won 9 and saved a league-leading 35 games. As one of baseball's top firemen, Lyle anchored the Yankee bull pen from 1976–78, when New York won three pennants.

Up in Boston, Cater batted only .237 his first year. He was then relegated to a pinch hitter's role until the Red Sox found a pigeon in St. Louis willing to trade for him.

Ferguson Jenkins for Bob Buhl and Larry Jackson

April 21, 1966

This is the only deal the Cubs made that let fans forget (at least momentarily) the infamous trade of Lou Brock for Ernie Broglio.

The Cubs actually pulled one over on someone else for a change. In this case, the Phillies were the victims. In exchange for Ferguson Jenkins and two other players, Philadelphia agreed to take weary-armed pitchers Bob Buhl and Larry Jackson, both at the tail end of their careers.

Jackson lasted three years, with a 41–45 record for the Phils. Buhl was even less useful. After compiling a 6–8 record, he retired.

In 1967, his first full season in Chicago, Jenkins won 20 games as the Cubs vaulted from tenth place to third.

For six straight seasons, Jenkins won 20 or more games, and the Cubs never finished lower than third. During that same stretch, the Phillies never placed higher than fifth.

SNOOZE PLAYS

The Most Mind-Boggling Mental Miscues

Major leaguers concentrate on every pitch, every batted ball, every play. Baloney! These guys daydream and get lost in their thoughts just like the rest of us working stiffs. The only problem is that their office is the playing field and when they get caught napping, they're in for a rude awakening. For "The Most Mind-boggling Mental Miscues," The Baseball Hall of SHAME inducts the following:

Cleveland Indians

July 25, 1983

No wonder the Cleveland Indians finished last in the American League East. Not only couldn't they win, but they showed thousands of fans they couldn't count, either.

They looked like kindergarten dropouts when, in the middle of a game, the entire team ran off the field with only two outs.

In the bottom of the sixth inning in a game against the Kansas City Royals, Cleveland pitcher Neal Heaton walked Hal McRae to start the frame and coaxed Amos Otis into grounding into a double play.

Then, to the amazement of everyone, Heaton walked toward the dugout, followed by the rest of the Indians, as if there were three outs. From the dugout, a chagrined and annoyed Indians manager Mike Ferraro, along with other players, shouted at the team to stay on the field. But the Tribe paid as much attention to them as they did to the scoreboard. Once they realized their folly, the players sheepishly returned to their positions and eventually lost 6–1. "How are you supposed to win a game when you don't know how many outs there are?" fumed Ferraro. "It's one thing to lose. It's another to look bad while doing it. I don't know where these guys have their heads, but it's not in the game."

Pee Wee Reese

Shortstop • Brooklyn, N.L. • July 12, 1947

Pee Wee Reese found to his everlasting embarrassment that courtesy has no business on the ball diamond.

In the bottom of the third inning of a home game against the Chicago Cubs, the Dodger shortstop was taking a lead off first base when batter Carl Furillo swung mightily and missed. The bat slipped out of Furillo's hands and sailed toward first base.

UPI/Bettmann Newsphotos

Being the nice guy that he was, Reese unthinkingly ambled off the bag to retrieve the bat. He left his brains behind. As the "Little Colonel" stooped down to pick up the bat, Cubs catcher Clyde McCullough fired the ball to first baseman Eddie Waitkus, who promptly tagged Reese out.

Reese should have known better. After all, he played for years under manager Leo Durocher, who always said, "Nice guys finish last."

Dick Bartell

Shortstop • Detroit, A.L. • Oct. 8, 1940

They called it "The $50,000 Snooze."

Dick Bartell, known for his heads-up play at shortstop, was caught with his head down at a crucial moment in the seventh and deciding game in the 1940 World Series.

His startling mental lapse cost the Detroit Tigers the world championship—and $50,000, the difference between their share of the winnings and that of the triumphant Cincinnati Reds.

The Tigers were winning 1–0 in the bottom of the seventh inning when Cincinnati's Frank McCormick doubled. The next batter, Jimmy Ripple, followed with another double. But McCormick, thinking the ball might be caught, held up for a few seconds. When the ball hit the wall, he started for third, slowed almost to a walk after rounding the bag, then took off for home.

Ordinarily, this would have been fatal. He would have been thrown out by 20 feet. But Bartell had his back turned as he received the throw from right fielder Bruce Campbell. The shortstop never bothered to turn around as McCormick headed toward the plate. The alarmed Tiger infield yelled frantically and waved their arms to wake Bartell up, but the little shortstop stood still, calmly turning the ball over and over in his paws while McCormick crossed the plate standing up for the tying run. Moments later, Ripple scored the winning run.

"I thought, of course, that McCormick was home long before I got the ball from Campbell and all I was thinking about was holding Ripple at second," Bartell said. "But I must have looked bad."

He sure did.

Lou Whitaker

Second baseman • Detroit, A.L. • July 16, 1985

Fans selected Lou Whitaker to start at second base in the 1985 All-Star Game for his glove and stick. He certainly wasn't chosen for his memory.

Whitaker arrived in Minneapolis ready to play, but with nothing to wear. In one of the most embarrassing mental blunders in mid-season classic history, the American League All-Star forgot to bring his uniform and gear. He left everything in the back seat of his Mercedes at home in Bloomfield Hills, Michigan.

An emergency effort to get a uniform flown in from Detroit failed when the replacement was lost in transit. So Whitaker was forced to dress up like a Little Leaguer.

He bought a Tigers jersey and cap from a Metrodome concession stand for $15 and a had a number 1 written in blue felt-tip pen on the back. He borrowed a pair of pants, and the Twins loaned him a pair of the team's blue socks.

The Mizuno company, which pays Whitaker $5,000 a year to wear its shoes, was on hand to present him with a pair of white shoes for the occasion. Finally, he borrowed a glove from Baltimore shortstop Cal Ripken, Jr. But Whitaker had to tape over the brand name because a rival company pays him $9,000 a year to wear *its* glove.

There was one item that no player was willing to share. Before the game Whitaker lamented, "I don't even have a protective cup."

Babe Herman

Outfielder • Cincinnati, N.L. • April 26, 1932

Once the game was over, Babe Herman's teammates left the day's trials and triumphs behind them at the ball park. But not Herman. He left behind his little boy.

Herman didn't mean to do it. He just plum forgot his 7-year-old son Bobby.

About six weeks after he had been traded by the Dodgers to the Reds, Herman was babysitting for Bobby; the outfielder's wife had remained in Brooklyn to look after their ill two-year-old son, Donny.

One day Herman took Bobby to a game at Crosley Field and told the boy to wait for him by the back of the stands after the game. Herman played great that day. Afterward, he happily showered, shaved, and dressed. Then, still on cloud nine, Herman hitched a ride home with his manager, Dan Howley.

Meanwhile, Bobby, being a good little boy, did what he was told and stood outside the ball park waiting for his no-show father.

When Herman was almost home, Howley turned to him and said, "Geeze, we left the kid!" Upon phoning the park, Herman was relieved to learn that the team secretary had found Bobby and was bringing him home.

Recalled Herman with a chuckle, "I guess I had too much on my mind that day."

George Brace Photo

34

EVERY TRICK IN THE BOOK

The Sneakiest Cheating Perpetrated by Players

To be a major leaguer, you first need to learn the basic fundamentals of the game, such as laying down a bunt, running the bases, and making the pivot on a double play. But to gain that extra edge that could mean the difference between winning and losing, players need to learn the finer points—how to doctor a bat, cut up a baseball, and other nifty, illegal tricks of the trade. For "The Sneakiest Cheating Perpetrated by Players," The Baseball Hall of SHAME inducts the following:

Baltimore Orioles

1893–99

The Baltimore Orioles didn't invent cheating, but they developed it into a precise science, earning a reputation as the dirtiest team in baseball history.

There was no trick in the book unknown to this rapscallion crew. Misguided by manager Ned Hanlon, crafty stars John McGraw, Willie Keeler, Wilbert Robinson, Hughey Jennings, and the rest of the conniving Orioles could fleece a con man out of his last dime.

They were blatant about pulling off their skulduggery at home games. If, during a Baltimore rally, a rival infielder was about to scoop up an easy grounder, he was suddenly blinded by an unexpected flash of light. Forced to turn his head away, he allowed the ball to skip past him for a hit. This was the insidious work of Oriole conspirators, who used hand mirrors to reflect the sun into the infielder's eyes.

Back then, foul balls hit into the stands or out of the park were returned. But in Baltimore, furtive fans threw back substitute balls that had been deadened by the Orioles. The next time such a doctored ball was hit—no matter how hard—by an opponent, it either blooped weakly into an infielder's glove or rolled dead near the pitcher's mound.

The players ordered head groundskeeper Tom Murphy to slope the third base foul line toward the infield so their bunts would curl fair.

Murphy was also told to keep the outfield grass so tall that it would resemble a rye field. This made it easy for the Orioles to hide a baseball or two for one of their patented tricks. Often, an opposing slugger hit a long drive that appeared to fly past a Baltimore outfielder. But the batter was held to only a single because the clever Oriole picked up one of the balls strategically hidden in the high grass and threw it back to the infield.

One time, however, the scheme backfired. Left fielder Joe Kelley made a perfect throw with a planted ball to shoot down a runner at third base, only to see center fielder Steve Brodie chase down the batted ball and fire it back to the infield, too.

Baltimore runners took advantage of the fact that games in those days were officiated by only one umpire, who stood in the middle of the field. When sprinting from first base to third, or second to home, the Orioles mastered the fine art of taking shortcuts across the diamond behind the back of the beleaguered umpire.

Enemy runners took their lives in their hands. As they tried to dash around the base paths, they were bumped, blocked, tripped, pushed, and spiked by the win-at-all-costs Orioles.

If a runner ever did make it to third, John McGraw used a little additional chicanery of his own to stop the foe from scoring. McGraw slipped his fingers through the runner's belt and held him just long enough to give a Baltimore fielder a better chance of throwing him out at the plate.

Once, in a game at Louisville, McGraw hooked his fingers inside the belt of Pete Browning, who was on third hoping to score. Tricking the trickster, Browning loosened his belt buckle. Then, on the next hit, he raced home, leaving a startled McGraw holding nothing but the belt.

Although Browning managed to put a temporary halt to that stunt, the Orioles could always pull another one out of their bag of dirty tricks.

Graig Nettles

Third baseman • New York, A.L. • Sept. 7, 1974

Graig Nettles' bat came unglued—and so did his tightly held secret.

In the fifth inning of a game against the visiting Detroit Tigers, the New York Yankees third baseman lofted a soft opposite-field single to left. Nettles hesitated for a moment before running to first because the end of his bat had fallen off.

Tiger catcher Bill Freehan chased after the broken piece of bat and brought it to home plate umpire Lou DiMuro. Freehan certainly knew an illegal cork-filled bat when he saw one because his teammate, first baseman Norm Cash, was particularly proud of his.

DiMuro examined Nettles' bat and found it plugged with cork, so he declared the bat illegal, the hit null, and Nettles out. Unfortunately, there was nothing the ump or the Tigers could do about Nettles' earlier second-inning home run, which had undoubtedly been hit with the same illegal bat. That homer produced the game's only run.

A close inspection of the bat after the game revealed that a two-inch piece had been sawed off the end. A hole had been drilled in the barrel and filled with cork. The end piece was then glued back onto the bat. With a corked center, the mass of a 36-ounce bat takes on the whiplash quickness of a 34-ouncer. A corked bat can add up to 50 feet to the distance a ball travels.

Nettles denied that he had tampered with the lumber. "I don't know what happened," he insisted, with a marvelously straight face, to reporters. "I didn't know there was anything wrong with the bat. That was the first time I used it. Some Yankee fan in Chicago gave it to me and said it would bring me good luck." It brought Nettles shame instead.

Preacher Roe

Pitcher • St. Louis-Pittsburgh-Brooklyn, N.L. • 1938, 1944–54

One of baseball's unwritten rules is "Do anything you can get away with." Preacher Roe followed that rule to the letter.

When the sneaky pitcher retired from the game, he boasted, "I threw spitballs the whole time I was with the Dodgers. Seven years in all. This isn't a confession and my conscience doesn't bother me a bit. Maybe the book says I was cheating, but I never felt that way."

Roe went a step beyond just talking about his cheating. In a 1955 *Sports Illustrated* article complete with photos, Roe revealed to the kids in America how to throw an illegal spitter.

As a pitcher for the Pittsburgh Pirates, Roe was going nowhere except to early showers. He suffered through two dismal seasons, 3–8 with an ERA of 5.14 in 1946, and 4–15 with an ERA of 5.25 the following year.

But his career made a dramatic turnaround in 1948 because of two changes in his life—he was traded to the Dodgers and he developed a spitball. He enjoyed six winning seasons, including a spectacular 22–3 mark in 1951, and recorded an ERA no higher than 3.30 during his first five years in Brooklyn.

Roe chomped on sticks of Beech-Nut chewing gum, which gave him the slick saliva he needed to load up the ball. When he pretended to wipe his brow, he quickly spit on the meaty part of his thumb. Then, as he hitched his belt, he moistened his middle fingers by rubbing them against his wet thumb. Placing his damp fingers on a seamless spot on the ball, he threw spitters that dropped just as they crossed the plate.

When he pitched, he wasn't the only one on his team to load up the ball. Once in a while, after the ball had been tossed around the infield, short-stop Pee Wee Reese or third baseman Billy Cox would come up to the mound, place the ball gently in Roe's glove and say, "There it is if you want it." That meant they already had spit on the ball.

Trying to sneak any advantage he could, Roe sometimes threw cut balls that would dipsey-do to the plate. Once, in 1954, when he was being relieved, Roe stood on the mound and cut the ball with his fingernail. He handed it to the new pitcher and said, "I've got a hole in that one if you want to use it. But you can get another ball if you want."

"Give it to me," Roe's teammate said eagerly. He proceeded to strike out the next batter on three straight pitches.

Philadelphia Phillies

1898

The Philadelphia Phillies resorted to an age-old scheme to steal signs from the opposing catcher—they used a spy.

Their undercover man was Morgan Murphy, a second-string catcher with a .198 batting average who nevertheless became one of the club's most valuable players. His teammates thought the stolen signals could improve their weak hitting.

Opponents did not know the Phils cheated until the Cincinnati Reds accidently uncovered the secret.

In a game at the Baker Bowl in Philadelphia, Reds shortstop and coach Tommy Corcoran was coaching at third base when his spikes got caught in what looked like a vine. He jerked it and several yards of wire popped out of the ground. Corcoran called time and traced the cable across the field to the Phillies' center field clubhouse.

Inside, Murphy was sitting by a little peephole with a telegraph set and binoculars. He had been stationed there so he could steal the signs from the opposing catcher. Murphy then tipped off the Phillies third base coach by means of a Morse-code buzzer system rigged up with underground wires. One buzz meant fastball, two meant a curve, and three was a slowball or change-up. Forewarned, the coach was able to signal the batter what pitch was coming.

Philly owner John I. Rogers thought this was perfectly fair and legitimate. The National League, however, declared that their little ruse was definitely unfair and illegitimate.

HITLESS WONDERS

The Most Inept Batting Performances

Every team is saddled with terrible hitters, guys who buy a round of drinks if they go 1-for-5. They hit for averages that aren't even good for bowling. Why, these players couldn't hit the floor if they fell out of bed. They would strike out trying to hit the ball off a T-ball stand. For "The Most Inept Batting Performances," The Baseball Hall of SHAME inducts the following:

Ray Oyler

Shortstop • Detroit-Seattle-Cleveland, A.L. • 1965–70

Ray Oyler was born an easy out. He lived in a slump his entire major league career, becoming the pitcher's best friend.

The shortstop, whose weak stick accounted for an appalling .175 lifetime average, batted only .135 in 1968, the lowest one-season mark ever for a major leaguer who has seen action in 100 or more games.

He was a remarkably good fielder but the fans in Detroit didn't seem to care about that. On Opening Day in 1968, the fans booed him as he ran onto the field with the starting lineup at Tiger Stadium.

Tigers fans just never appreciated Oyler the way the Seattle Pilots fans did the following year. When he stepped to the plate for his first at-bat in a Seattle uniform, horns blew, confetti flew, signs fluttered, and the first meeting of the Ray Oyler Fan Club had come to order.

Oyler's fan club was the brainchild of KVI Radio disc jockey Bob Hardwick. He was looking over the list of players for whom the Pilots had paid $175,000 each in the American League expansion draft when his eyes stopped short at Oyler's .135 batting average.

This wasn't much bang for the buck, Hardwick reasoned, and here was a guy who obviously needed help. So the Ray Oyler Fan Club was founded. By the first month of the season, more than 5,000 members had joined. The only requirement was a horn, enthusiasm, and "an abiding faith in the power of positive thinking."

Their joy turned to outrage when their hero was decked in a fight against Kansas City's Jim Campanis on April 22, 1969. Fan club president

Hardwick sent an angry telegram to Royals general manager Cedric Tallis which said, in part: "Five thousand members of the Ray Oyler Fan Club protest the slugging of our beloved leader. Please do not misinterpret our club motto, 'Sock it to Ray Oyler,' as this is an expression of encouragement."

The loyalty of the Seattle fans inspired the slender 165-pound shortstop. That year he hit his weight, literally.

Johnny Broaca

Pitcher • New York-Cleveland, A.L. • 1934–39

To Johnny Broaca, batting was like an IRS audit—you don't want to go, but you have no choice.

Broaca simply hated to bat.

"I've never seen anything like it," said former batting star George Kell. "No player ever would pass up a chance to hit morning, noon, or night—not even if he couldn't hit his hat size."

Broaca would indeed pass up the chance. Even on the days he was scheduled to pitch, Broaca holed up in the clubhouse rather than go out and take his licks in the batting cage.

Naturally, this incredible aversion to hitting was reflected in his batting average. During his six years in the bigs, Broaca made 254 trips to the plate, somehow collected 23 hits, and left baseball with a horrendous .091 lifetime average.

His first hit was really an accident. In a game against the Senators on July 1, 1934, Broaca assumed his usual stance at the plate, his bat firmly planted on his shoulder. The pitch sailed high and inside and glanced off the bat that still rested on Broaca's shoulder. To everyone's astonishment— especially Broaca's—the ball caromed over third base for a hit.

A week earlier, Broaca had etched his name in the record books. Thanks to his severe batting allergy, Broaca broke out with a record-tying rash of strikeouts when he batted against the White Sox on June 25. Five times he trudged up to the plate. Five times he retreated to the safety of the dugout after striking out.

He was a little premature on one strikeout. While doing his imitation of a statue in the batter's box, Broaca ran the count to 2–2. Before the next pitch was called by umpire George Moriarty, Broaca—hoping and assuming it was strike three—turned away and marched back to the dugout and sat down.

Mystified, Moriarty wandered over. "I'm sorry, Johnny," the ump said. "That was ball three. You'll have to come back."

Hank Aguirre

Pitcher • Cleveland-Detroit, A.L.;
Los Angeles-Chicago, N.L. • 1955–70

All pitchers have a license to be lousy hitters, but Hank Aguirre deserved to have his revoked.

In nine of his 16 seasons in the bigs, he batted under .100, and went hitless in five of those years. In 388 at-bats, he struck out 68 percent of the time, and collected only 33 hits for an abysmal lifetime average of .085.

Aguirre was so pathetic at the plate that when he finally got his first hit after going 0-for-2 years, the fans gave him a long standing ovation.

It happened in his eighth season. The Detroit Tigers had tried everything they could think of to put some muscle in his weak swing. He took extra batting practice, followed special coaching instructions, and studied films of himself. He even accepted a coach's offer of a free steak dinner if he'd get a hit.

One thing Aguirre hadn't tried was batting left handed. In a game against the Yankees at Tiger Stadium on June 22, 1962, Aguirre swatted from the southpaw side of the plate for the first time in his life. Lo and behold, he hit a soft drive that fell into short right field for an RBI single! The 43,723 fans went wild. They stood and cheered for a full five minutes in an ovation that even Mickey Mantle had never heard.

"My gosh, I've been batting the wrong way my entire life!" declared Aguirre, whose batting average soared from .000 to an awesome .009.

(Actually, Aguirre did get a hit the week before. He smacked a tennis ball to left field for a double in a father-son game.)

After the Yankee game, sportswriters crowded around Aguirre. "I figured I'd win the MHH Award for most horrible hitting," he said. "Now maybe they'll let me order some bats with my own name on them."

It didn't matter what bat he used or which side of the plate he swung from because he collected only one more hit the rest of the year. "I think my hitting is progressing," he said at the time. "It's becoming progressively worse."

Nevertheless, he did enjoy one great moment on June 4, 1967, and once again it was against the Yankees. Pitcher Fritz Peterson had intentionally walked Ray Oyler, a .186 hitter, to load the bases and get at Hammerless Hank. Aguirre took two quick strikes and then somehow managed to slam the first triple of his life.

After sliding into third base, the exuberant Aguirre whispered to coach Tony Cuccinello, "I'm gonna steal home." Cooch shook his head and said, "Hank, it took you 13 years to get here, so don't fool around."

Ron Herbel

Pitcher • San Francisco-San Diego-New York-Atlanta, N.L. • 1963–71

Ron Herbel deserved to be poster child for the designated hitter rule.

The bespectacled, right-handed pitcher had no business touching a bat, let alone swinging one. He holds the record for the lowest career batting average of anyone who has batted at least 100 times—a shamefully microscopic .029. Herbel went hitless in five seasons, topped by an 0-for-47 mark in 1964 that ranks as the third worst single year in major league history.

After 56 attempts, Herbel banged out his first hit in the Astrodome on May 21, 1965, giving him an excuse to expound on his batting technique to reporters. "In the minors," he said, "once in a while I'd close my eyes and get a hit. The pitcher would usually have to hit my bat, though."

Herbel would have collected his second hit, this time in Wrigley Field, on September 4, 1965, had he known what to do. So surprised was Herbel at rapping a clean shot to right field that he forgot to run fast enough and was thrown out at first base by Cubs right fielder Billy Williams.

He got his next hit the following year, in the Astrodome, prompting the Giants publicity department to banner his hitting, or rather lack of it. In the 1967 media guide, a footnote to Herbel's statistics mentioned that his only two hits in 134 at-bats had been indoors. "I've never heard of a pitcher's batting record included in a club's press guide," Herbel groused. "Somebody really knows how to hurt a guy."

Herbel finally garnered his first outdoor hit, a ground-rule double no less, on April 16, 1967. That's the good news. The bad news is that he got picked off second on the very next play.

PARTING SHOTS

The Most Outrageous Behavior When Leaving a Game

When players are yanked out of the game by the manager after a poor performance, they often pout or scowl as they stalk off the field. However, these acts are nothing more than hackneyed baseball theatrics. A truly deplorable departure features a flair for showmanship—a parting shot that turns into a classic melodramatic spectacle. For "The Most Outrageous Behavior When Leaving a Game," The Baseball Hall of SHAME inducts the following:

Wes Ferrell

Pitcher • Cleveland-Boston-Washington-New York, A.L.; Brooklyn-Boston, N.L. • 1927–41

Wes Ferrell made more graceless exits from games than any other pitcher in baseball.

Often, when he was given the hook, Ferrell refused to leave the mound until he finished throwing one of his patented temper tantrums. Other times, he stalked off the mound without warning in the middle of an inning.

No flare-up caused him more trouble than the one he triggered on August 30, 1932. Pitching for the Cleveland Indians against the Boston Red Sox at Fenway Park, Ferrell gave up two runs, three hits, and a walk while getting only two outs in the first inning.

Cleveland manager Roger Peckinpaugh had seen enough. After he strode to the mound and signaled for relief pitcher Jack Russell, Peckinpaugh told Ferrell to take a shower. Ferrell threw off his cap and vigorously shook his head no. Then he kept turning his back to his manager, who had to circle the mound in an attempt to face the obstinate pitcher.

When Russell arrived, Ferrell kicked up dirt and refused to give his teammate the ball. Finally, Peckinpaugh wrestled the ball away from Ferrell, who stomped off the field talking to himself. For this bout of insubordination, Ferrell was suspended without pay for 10 days.

Four years later, when he was pitching for the Red Sox, Ferrell was suspended again and fined—only this time it was for taking himself out of a game in the middle of an inning without permission. Actually, he was punished for walking out on his teammates two games in a row.

After giving up a cheap three-run double in a game against the Washington Senators on August 16, 1936, Ferrell suddenly walked off the mound. His unexpected departure caught manager Joe Cronin completely by surprise. Because he had no pitcher warming up in the bull pen, Cronin had to stall. He called Mel Almada in from the outfield under the pretense of giving him a new shoelace. This gave relief pitcher Jack Russell a few more minutes to loosen up.

A week later, on August 21, in a game against the New York Yankees, Ferrell made another unauthorized exit. With two out in the bottom of the sixth inning of a 1–1 tie, Ferrell gave up three runs on three hits and two walks and couldn't get the third out. So he stormed off the mound. Cronin ran out of the dugout and yelled at his pitcher to return to his position, but the headstrong hurler paid him no heed.

Cronin was outraged, and announced that Ferrell had been suspended and fined $1,000. When a reporter told Ferrell the news, the pitcher declared, "I'm going to slug that Irishman right on his lantern jaw!" The reporter relayed the message to Cronin, who retorted, "If he wants to slug me, I'll be passing through the hotel lobby at six o'clock on my way to dinner."

Cronin was there. Ferrell was not.

Reggie Jackson

Outfielder • New York, A.L. • June 18, 1977

As a nationwide TV audience watched the Red Sox battle the Yankees for first place, Reggie Jackson drew all the attention in a pitiful melodrama of his own making.

First, he acted like a little old lady when he let a fly ball drop in right field. His manager and number one critic, Billy Martin, panned the performance and yanked him from the game. For an encore, Jackson played a crybaby while Martin portrayed a bully.

The histrionics were performed in the bottom of the sixth inning with the Yankees losing 7–4. Boston's Jim Rice lofted a check-swing fly ball to right field. Rather than run in for the catch, Jackson loafed on the ball and let it fall in front of him. After taking his sweet time to pick it up, he threw weakly in the general direction of the pitcher's mound. Rice ended up with an inexcusably cheap double.

Livid with rage, Martin sent Paul Blair out to right field to replace Jackson. The TV cameras followed Jackson as he ran into the dugout. Humiliated in front of his viewing public, Jackson waved his arms wildly at Billy and shouted, "What's going on? What did I do?"

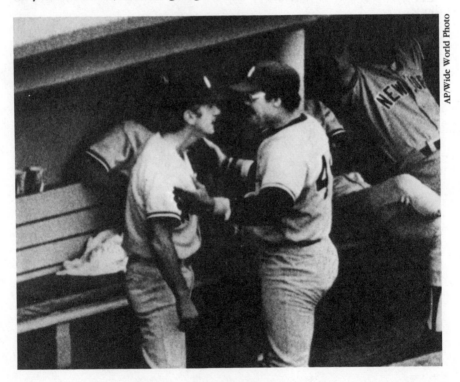

AP/Wide World Photo

"You didn't hustle!" Martin yelled back.

"You showed me up!" Jackson screamed. "You have to be crazy to embarrass me in front of 50 million people. How could you do this to me on television? You don't know what you're doing, old man."

Somebody should have told Reggie he was saying the wrong lines. First, he deserved to be lifted because he dallied after the ball in a crucial game. Second, he was more concerned about his public image than he was about the team's welfare. And third, he called Martin an *old man.*

Martin needed no script for this scene. He responded in the only way he knew how. But coaches Elston Howard and Yogi Berra grabbed him before he had a chance to belt Jackson.

"You never liked me!" Jackson shouted as he stormed into the clubhouse. "You never did want me on the ball club. Well, I'm here to stay, so you better start liking me."

This whole performance deserved three strikes.

Frank LaCorte

Pitcher • Houston, N.L. • May 26, 1982

Burned up over yet another of his lousy pitching performances, Frank LaCorte stalked off the mound and into the clubhouse for a parting shot that went up in smoke—he torched his uniform.

In a home game against the Montreal Expos, the Houston Astros relief pitcher started the tenth inning of a 0–0 game by walking three batters in a row. LaCorte, who had yet to win a game that year, was summarily yanked. By the time he plopped down in front of his locker, his reliever had given up a run-producing sacrifice fly and a three-run homer for a 4–0 Astros loss.

LaCorte was flaming mad and had to do something to vent his rage. After several previous poor outings, he had destroyed clubhouse trash cans and broken teammates' bats. This time he stripped off his uniform, pulled out a book of matches, and set fire to his jersey.

Slumped over the charred remains, LaCorte told reporters, "That jersey took a long time to burn. Took a lot of matches. It doesn't burn easily but it burns long."

Then he requested a new number from the club. He didn't want number 31 anymore because he was tired of running up so many 3-and-1 counts. He received a new number (27) and a new jersey—and a $250 fine for burning his old uniform.

The new number didn't help him much. LaCorte won only once all year. The season was so bad that during one game his own son turned on him. "Frank," shouted little 4-year-old Vince LaCorte from his Astrodome box seat, "throw a damn strike!"

Russ "Mad Monk" Meyer

Pitcher • Brooklyn, N.L. • May 24, 1953

It was a game that tested Mad Monk Meyer's temper. He failed.

The hotheaded hurler was pitching well against the Phillies at Connie Mack Stadium. But in the fifth inning, bad luck struck him down. His Dodger teammates botched a couple of plays, and the Phillies swatted three broken-bat hits in a row to put Meyer in deep trouble.

Brooklyn manager Chuck Dressen decided to make a pitching change. It always took an act of bravery to remove Meyer, so Dressen used a little cunning. He caught Meyer off guard by waiting until there was a 2-and-0 count on the next hitter. Then Dressen called time and strolled out toward the mound as if he were just going to chat with his pitcher.

Suddenly, Dressen's arm shot up, signaling for a reliever. Knowing the explosiveness of the Mad Monk, the umpires sprang into action like a SWAT team at a hostage crisis. The four arbiters closed in on the mound in a show of force.

Meyer was out of the game—but he wasn't going to go quietly. In a rage, he grabbed the resin bag and threw it straight up in the air with all his might. But he forgot that what goes up must come down. As he stormed at Dressen, the bag fell down and beaned Meyer right on top of the head. He ended up looking like the Pillsbury doughboy after a weekend binge.

Boom-Boom Beck

Pitcher • Brooklyn, N.L. • July 4, 1934

It was a typical day on the mound for Dodger pitcher Boom-Boom Beck. Hitters were smashing shots off him as if he were lobbing tennis balls. Line drives banged off the close, tin, right field wall at Philadelphia's Baker Bowl, sounding like target practice.

This not only made Boom-Boom ornery, but also irked his right fielder Hack Wilson, as well, since the hard-drinking veteran was nursing a hangover.

Finally, manager Casey Stengel had seen enough. He trudged to the mound and told Beck he was through. Enraged at the thought of an early shower, Boom-Boom refused to hand the ball over to Stengel. This perplexed the Ol' Perfessor, who figured that Beck, a 20-game loser the previous year, should have been used to getting the hook.

Instead of giving Stengel the ball, the short-tempered Boom-Boom whirled and fired the ball as hard as he could. It hit the right field wall with a resounding boom.

Meanwhile, Wilson, who hadn't paid any attention to Beck's antics, was in his own little world. With his hands on his knees, he was catching his breath and reflecting on the evils of demon rum.

Suddenly awakened by the sound of the ball ricocheting off the tin wall, Wilson sprang into action like a Pavlovian dog. He tracked down the ball, as he had so many others, and fired a perfect strike to the startled second baseman. Too bad it didn't count. It was, said Stengel, the best throw Wilson made all year.

John Montefusco

Pitcher • San Francisco, N.L. • June 18, 1980

He proudly calls himself "The Count." But John Montefusco went down for the count after raising a big stink over being relieved.

Beating the Mets in the ninth inning, Montefusco began to tire as New York launched a last-ditch threat. So Giants manager Dave Bristol, just doing his job, decided to make a pitching change.

The Count complained and pouted before finally stalking off the mound, sorry behavior for a major leaguer. But he saved his disgraceful parting shot for after the game, which the Giants won 8–5.

Not content to end the day a winner on the field, Montefusco became a loser in the clubhouse. He barged into Bristol's office, triggering a nasty fight. The Count came out with a black eye.

But at least he got in the last word. He told reporters, "I had Bristol in a headlock and was about to beat the crap out of him when we were separated."

This was the same guy who had had the audacity to blame his manager after throwing a game-tying gopher ball. In a game in 1976, Montefusco had a two-run lead over the Montreal Expos in the eighth inning when he gave up a homer with a man on. Giants manager Bill Rigney yanked him. The Count ran to the press and complained, "The manager is a loser and he's dragging me down with him."

It sounded just like a line from the lips of Ring Lardner's character Alibi Ike.

THE REAR END OF THE FRONT OFFICE

The Most Disgraceful Actions by Owners

Baseball owners and dictators are much alike. They can do what they want—who's going to stop them? The only difference between the two is that owners last longer. There are no armed revolts in baseball. With no one to answer to, owners have hatched outrageous schemes out of greed, ignorance, or nastiness. For "The Most Disgraceful Actions by Owners," The Baseball Hall of SHAME inducts the following:

Walter O'Malley

Brooklyn-Los Angeles, N.L. • 1951–70

Walter O'Malley was one of the tightest of the tightwads in baseball. Even though he had deep pockets, he made Scrooge look like Santa Claus with a blank check.

The Dodger owner displayed his greedy side for all to see in 1962. When he built Dodger Stadium, he deliberately eliminated drinking fountains to boost sales of beer and soft drinks. On Opening Day, April 10, 1962, one thirsty reporter noted ruefully that the only two drinking fountains in the $22 million stadium were in the dugouts.

To this revelation, O'Malley, through a spokesman, replied that there were 221 cold water faucets in 48 bathrooms at the stadium. But, as *Los Angeles Times* columnist Jim Murray pointed out, "Who wants to hang like a sloth from the wall to get a drink of water?"

The City Health Department intervened, directing O'Malley to place 11 drinking fountains in the stadium's preferred seating areas and two in the bleachers.

O'Malley stuck it not only to the fans but also to his tenants, the Los Angeles Angels, a new expansion team that played at Dodger Stadium from 1962–65. Angels owner Gene Autry, who counted O'Malley as a good friend, discovered to his dismay that kindly old Walter was cheating him.

An Angel accountant noticed that while the rich and successful Dodgers were drawing 76 percent of the customers into the stadium, O'Malley was charging the Angels for 50 percent of the toilet paper used in the ball park.

Before long, Autry's accountant came up with proof that O'Malley was billing the Angels for fictitious items like "cleaning office windows," when in fact the Angels front office worked out of windowless rooms in the stadium basement.

On still another day, Autry learned that he was paying for the care and watering of the stadium grass when his club was home. Autry, who was also in the hotel business, told a reporter, "I'd have a hell of a time getting people who rent my rooms to water the posies. That's the responsibility of the landlord."

So Autry took his team and ran off to Anaheim, where the folks built him a shiny new stadium that he didn't have to share with a cheapskate.

Autry need not have taken O'Malley's stinginess personally. Walter's own players were victims of his niggardly ways. Like other owners in championship years, O'Malley rewarded his team with rings as World Series mementoes. Whenever the Dodgers won again, their boss gave them new rings—but only after he first collected the old ones.

Judge Emil Fuchs

Boston, N.L. • 1923–35

Boston Braves owner Judge Emil Fuchs knew little about baseball—and to prove it, he appointed himself manager in 1929.

"A manager must no longer chew tobacco and talk out of the side of his mouth," declared the Judge. "The club can't do any worse with me as manager than it has done the past few years."

The pronouncement was not among the Judge's best. He made a bad team worse; the Braves fell from seventh to last place.

The likeable, squat millionaire and former New York magistrate had once been a semi-pro catcher of limited skills. He felt this experience was adequate enough for him to pilot a major league team.

However, the players quicky recognized Fuchs's shortcomings and paid little attention to his signals from the bench. They usually went along with instructions from third base coach Johnny Evers. It wasn't long before all of Boston tittered over the Fuchs Funnies.

UPI/Bettmann Newsphotos

When shortstop Rabbit Maranville suggested to Fuchs that he order a squeeze play during a close game, Fuchs replied, "I'll do nothing of the kind. We'll win this game honorably or not at all."

On another occasion, Evers stopped a game and walked over to the dugout where Fuchs was in the middle of telling a story to his players. "The count is 3-and-1 on the batter," Evers informed the manager. "What do you want him to do?"

The Judge interrupted his story long enough to say, "Tell him to hit a home run."

On one rare occasion when the Braves had a robust lead, the talkative boss-manager was unraveling a lengthy yarn to his bench warmers. Five minutes later, pitcher Art Delaney, who was sitting in the dugout, interrupted Fuchs. "Hey, Judge, they've tied the score, the bases are full and there's nobody out. Better get a pitcher ready."

"Oh, yes," said Fuchs, a bit irritated at the interruption. "Run down to the bull pen, Art, and get warmed up. I'll tell you the rest of the story when you get back."

Fuchs wasn't very successful in the front office either. During his 13-year reign as owner, the Braves finished in the second division 11 times. Fuchs nearly sent his fellow club owners into an apoplectic fit when he proposed to run dog races in Braves Field. The outcry was strong enough for him to reconsider.

A millionaire going into baseball, Fuchs bowed out of the game nearly bankrupt. "I lost over one million dollars in my venture in major league baseball," he said. "I have no regrets." But Braves fans did.

C. Arnholt Smith

San Diego, N.L. • 1969–74

Under the reign of millionaire wheeler-dealer C. Arnholt Smith, the San Diego Padres were condemned to a Machiavellian hell.

He sanctioned an unofficial "department of dirty tricks," which was known for using lie detector tests on personnel and bugging phone conversations of players' union activities.

Smith made the baseball establishment wince when he began picking players based on their scores on team-administered personality tests and other computerized data. A player's ego, psyche, intelligence, demeanor, and even grammar were computed along with fielding, hitting, running, and throwing ability. Smith never did explain what knowledge of Shakespeare had to do with swinging a bat or what proper diction had to do with throwing a curve.

The brains behind this bird-brained scheme were team executive Peter

Bavasi and San Jose State University professor Bruce Ogilvie. Based on their charts and tests, the Padres drafted Eli Borunda, who, the scores suggested, would develop into a fine strikeout pitcher. He ended up pitching not baseballs but religion as a door-to-door evangelist.

Because of the test scores, the Padres picked Mike Ivie to be the catcher the team so desperately needed. Ivie was paid $100,000 before the team discovered something that didn't show up on the personality test—Ivie couldn't throw the ball back to the pitcher. Oh, he could throw fine to first, second, or third, but when he tossed the ball back toward the mound, it hit the pitcher on the shins or sailed over his head.

John McNamara scored high on the tests and was made manager in 1974. He lasted until early in the 1977 season, never leading the team out of the second division.

The Padres looked as bad as they played. Smith insisted they wear brown uniforms. In fact, everything had to be brown, from the blazers worn by front-office personnel to the paper they wrote on. It was his color. Smith rode around in brown Cadillacs and wore only brown suits, hats, and shoes.

But his biggest concern was the green. He put the Padres on a poverty budget so piddling that the team couldn't even pick up bargain basement waiver-price ball players. That's because the multimillionaire was hard up for cash.

Throughout his tenure, he secretly juggled millions of dollars to keep afloat an empire that included the Padres, an airline, a taxi company, a hotel, a bank, and a tuna fleet. He tried desperately to stay one step ahead of the IRS, the Securities and Exchange Commission, and the FBI. He lost the race, along with a $200 million bank and the San Diego Padres.

Frank Farrell and Bill Devery

New York, A.L. • 1903–14

If Frank Farrell and Bill Devery tried to enter the baseball establishment today, they'd be taken by the scruffs of their necks and thrown out at the doorstep.

The very first owners of the New York Yankees were shady characters and Tammany Hall alumni. They were as crooked as loaded dice.

Farrell was a professional gambler who owned race horses, ran gambling houses, and operated disreputable enterprises. Farrell's business associates were bookies, cops on the take, crooked politicians, gamblers, and other plungers. His political associations dated back to the days when he owned a saloon on the lower west side. Furthermore, he was the kingpin in a syndicate that operated the majority of pool houses and gambling joints in New York.

Farrell persistently denied that he had anything to do with gambling, yet the newspapers featured stories and photos of his gambling houses, including a lavish one open to "those who have thousands to lose." Devery, once chief of police, was repeatedly accused of graft and corruption. He became wealthy by being "bag man" for one of the Tammany bosses.

Farrell and Devery bought the franchise of the defunct Baltimore club for $18,000 and moved it to New York in 1903. They knew absolutely nothing about baseball yet, like wiley poker players, they bluffed the baseball world.

They harassed their manager, Clark Griffith, one of the craftiest tacticians in the game, and they had the temerity to question him on the way he ran the team. Griffith quit—as did six other managers under Farrell and Devery.

The team was short on leadership and long on odds. During the Farrell-Devery ownership, the Yankees never won a pennant and finished fifth or lower eight times. It was a sure bet Farrell and Devery would end up losers. And they did.

Brad Corbett

Texas, A.L. • 1974–80

No one who tried to buy himself a world championship did so more stupidly or more recklessly than Texas Rangers owner Brad Corbett.

He jumped into contract negotiations with both hands and both feet, but forgot his head. He was baseball's biggest pigeon. Like swindlers out to fleece an easy mark, agents, players, and fellow owners couldn't wait to do business with the impulsive owner. As a result, he cut some of the worst deals in the game, buying nothing but trouble deep in the heart of Texas.

The portly cigar chomper, who made his fortune running a plastic pipe company, dropped millions of his own hard-earned cash to make millionaires out of has-beens and never-would-be's. Then, as often as not, he dumped them.

In 1977, Corbett handed slugger Richie Zisk a 10-year, $2.95 million contract to leave the White Sox. He traded him three years later. That same winter, Corbett landed shortstop Bert Campaneris for $1 million. Campy rewarded the owner's generosity by hitting .186 in 1978 and was sent packing.

Before the 1978 season, Corbett awarded pitcher Bert Blyleven a $2 million, 22-year contract. Despite the fact that the Rangers had Blyleven under contract until the year 2,000, they traded him to Pittsburgh days later. In the middle of the 1979 season, Corbett dealt away the Rangers' top hitter, Oscar Gamble, to the Yankees. A few weeks later, the pinstriped Gamble smashed a game-winning grand slam homer against his old team.

In a 1979 newspaper poll of agents, Corbett's negotiating skills were voted "totally off the wall." One agent said he enjoyed doing business with Corbett more than anyone else because "you almost always get your money out of him."

Corbett learned you can't buy happiness or a pennant (unless you're George Steinbrenner, in which case you can only buy a pennant).

On the night of July 4, 1977, Corbett wandered into the Arlington Stadium press box during a game, broke into tears, and called his players "dogs on the field and dogs off the field." He later berated them in the clubhouse. That's because the only thing the Rangers did well was mosey up to the pay window on the first and the fifteenth of the month and collect paychecks that would make J.R. Ewing blanch.

By the start of the 1980 season, Corbett had unloaded 12 players from the previous year's team. A Dallas newspaper polled its readers on "What's wrong with the Rangers?" To no one's surprise, Corbett was the over-whelming choice.

When the press pointed out the folly of his negotiating, he railed at the sportswriters and threatened to sell the team "to some Arabs."

The fans were fed up with his awful deals. During a home game on August 27, 1979, many in the crowd brandished T-shirts that read, "Trade Chuckles the Clown," their derisive nickname for Corbett. Meanwhile, another group of fans stood underneath the owner's box shouting obsceni-ties at him. Corbett tried placating the fans by throwing them baseballs. They threw them back.

Run for Your Lives!

The Most Outrageous Base-Running Fiascoes

Some players are such horrendous runners they could use a second base coach. It's not that their legs are slow so much as it is their minds are working at only quarter speed. To others, running the base paths can be as reckless and foolish as strolling down a dark alley at midnight. For "The Most Outrageous Base-Running Fiascoes," The Baseball Hall of SHAME inducts the following:

Ollie O'Mara

Shortstop • Brooklyn, N.L. • 1916

Somewhere between home plate and first base, Ollie O'Mara lost his mind.

In a game against the New York Giants, the Brooklyn Dodgers had

George Brace Photo

runners Hy Myers on first base and Jack Coombs on second when O'Mara stepped up to the plate with orders to bunt. O'Mara dropped a slow roller along the third base line. Catcher Bill Rariden grabbed the ball, but threw wildly to third, trying to catch Coombs coming from second. Almost immediately, Rariden yelled, "Foul Ball!" He hoped to wipe out his error by tricking umpire Bill Klem into thinking the ball wasn't fair.

O'Mara had started for first, but turned around and headed back toward the batter's box after he heard someone shout that it was a foul.

But Klem yelled, "Fair ball!"

O'Mara, oblivious to the errant throw, bellowed back, "Foul ball!"

Klem insisted otherwise and thundered, "Fair ball!"

Meanwhile, left fielder George Burns was chasing the ball, which had by now rolled all the way to the fence. As O'Mara continued to argue with the umpire, four Dodgers jumped out of the dugout, raced up to O'Mara, and exhorted him to start running. But the hardheaded O'Mara refused to listen to them and remained at the plate.

While the debate raged, base runners Coombs and Myers scored, and Burns tracked down the ball. In desperation, the Brooklyn strong-arm squad grabbed O'Mara and hustled him down the first base line as he kicked, punched, and screamed at his teammates.

It was all to no avail. The protesting O'Mara and his escorts were thrown out at first base by ten feet.

Dan Ford

Outfielder • Minnesota, A.L. • Sept. 5, 1978

Minnesota Twins manager Gene Mauch furiously paced around his office and declared, "All I've got to say is that the man will not get paid for tonight's game."

His ire was directed at Twins center fielder Dan Ford, who committed the dumbest base-running blunder that the veteran manager—and most baseball observers—had ever seen.

Minnesota was losing to the visiting Chicago White Sox 4–0 in the bottom of the seventh inning when the Twins loaded the bases with Ford on third, Jose Morales on second, and Larry Wolfe on first. When Bombo Rivera lined a one-out single to center, Ford backpeddled down the third base line, waving his arms and yelling "C'mon, Jose! C'mon Jose!" to Morales, who was trying to score from second.

The problem with such cheerleading was that Ford stopped short of home plate and continued to urge on his teammate, who then flew past him and touched home. Suddenly, Ford realized that *he* hadn't crossed the plate, and immediately touched it with his toe. But White Sox catcher Bill Nahorodny noticed the mixup and shouted at umpire Joe Brinkman, who called Morales out for passing Ford.

Mauch ran out of the dugout and, with a resigned look on his face, asked Brinkman, "Did what I think happened, happen?" The ump nodded. Mauch turned away without protest. As he headed back to the dugout with the downcast and embarrassed Ford, Mauch growled, "Just keep right on going." Ford went straight into the clubhouse and left the stadium before the end of the game.

Instead of two runs and one out, the Twins had one run and two outs. The play took on added importance because Minnesota lost 4–3.

That wasn't the only time Ford blundered badly on the base paths that year. In a game against the Detroit Tigers, Ford was motoring from first to third on a single. The throw from the outfield was way off, forcing third baseman Aurelio Rodriguez to scamper 15 feet from the base to make the catch.

Ford would have made it safely to third—if only he had slid into the base instead of into Rodriguez.

Bobby Meacham
Shortstop

Dale Berra
Third baseman

New York, A.L. • Aug. 2, 1985

Lou Gehrig
First Baseman

Dixie Walker
Outfielder

New York, A.L. • April 29, 1933

The baseball Hall of SHAME would be remiss if it did not grant special dishonor to four New York Yankees who proved that history—no matter how unbelievable—does repeat itself.

In the most astounding base running fiasco ever witnessed at Yankee Stadium, Bobby Meacham and Dale Berra were tagged out in bang-bang succession at home plate on the same play. Incredibly, this rare basepath blunder was not the first committed by the Yankees. Fifty-two years earlier, in an almost identical botch-up, stars Lou Gehrig and Dixie Walker ran into the same double trouble at home plate.

In both cases, the boneheaded play cost the Yankees a chance at victory. While the old-time pinstripers embarrassed themselves before 36,000 fans, Berra and Meacham humiliated themselves in front of millions on national television.

Meacham was on second base and Berra on first in the seventh inning of a 3–3 tie with the visiting Chicago White Sox when teammate Rickey Henderson smacked a booming drive to left-center field. It should have been a two-run double. But the mighty blow turned into a 400-foot, double-play single.

Meacham, waiting to see if the ball would be caught, held at second while Berra, believing the ball would fall, took off from first. As the ball hit the ground, Meacham stumbled, and then headed for third with Berra right on his heels.

When they reached third, coach Gene Michael waved Meacham home. But Berra, thinking what was good enough for Meacham was good enough for him, also sprinted around third, causing Michael to throw his arms in the air in confusion. Waiting at the plate was catcher Carlton Fisk, who caught a perfect relay throw. Fisk tagged out Meacham in a collision and then spun around to tag Berra. It was your typical 8-to-6-to-2-to-2 play.

New York manager Billy Martin was so upset at Berra that he benched him on the spot. The startling double play ruined a Yankee scoring threat and the team lost 6–5 in 11 innings. Fumed Martin, "I've never seen a play like that in grammar school, let alone the major leagues."

That's because Martin wasn't even five years old when Lou Gehrig and Dixie Walker pulled the same base-running boner.

It happened when the Yankees were losing to the Washington Senators 6–3 in the bottom of the ninth. With Gehrig on second base and Walker on first, Tony Lazzeri walloped a shot to right-center field. Like Rickey Henderson's drive, Lazzeri's potential two-run double turned into a shocking 400-foot, double-play single.

Thinking the ball might be caught, Gehrig cautiously hugged second while Walker, head down, sprinted from first. When the ball fell safely, Gehrig took off and rounded third only a few feet ahead of Walker. The two looked like track team members ready to exchange the baton as they dashed for home.

Meanwhile, catcher Luke Sewell caught the relay throw and, grinning like a Cheshire cat, waited for his victims. Gehrig tried to score standing up and smashed into Sewell, but the catcher held onto the ball and tagged him out. Then Sewell dove at Walker and tagged him as well for a shameful double play that wasn't repeated for more than a half century.

Willie Stargell

First baseman • Pittsburgh, N.L. • Sept. 19, 1978

Willie Stargell couldn't believe his eyes. Pittsburgh Pirates manager Chuck Tanner had given him the steal sign.

Stargell, whose legs could hardly shift from neutral to first gear, stole bases about as often as an eclipse of the sun. But on this particular day, with the Pirates romping over the Chicago Cubs at Wrigley Field, he thought, "Who am I to argue with Tanner?"

So Stargell lumbered toward second in one of the most ridiculous base-stealing attempts ever seen in the majors.

The paunchy, 38-year-old veteran ran as fast as he could, but even his own shadow had passed him. When Stargell was about two-thirds of the way to second, he began a slide that made him look more like a beached whale than a ball player.

He came to a dead stop about 10 feet from the bag. Closing in on the prone runner, Cubs shortstop Ivan DeJesus was about to make an easy tag. Stargell, who thought much quicker than he ran, decided there was only one possible way out of this predicament. He stood up, formed a "T" with his hands, and shouted, "Time out!" The only "out" the umpire called was Stargell.

He returned to a dugout that was rollicking with laughter. After a teammate had regained his composure, he asked Stargell why he slid so soon. "I was given some bad information," answered Stargell with a straight face. "I was told the bases were only seventy feet apart."

Gary Geiger

Outfielder • Boston, A.L. • June 8, 1961

Gary Geiger went from hero to zero in a matter of seconds. He hit what he thought was a game-winning triple. Unfortunately, it wasn't.

In a lengthy night game against the visiting Los Angeles Angels, the Boston Red Sox entered the bottom of the eleventh inning losing 4–3. But leadoff hitter Chuck Schilling walked, and Geiger smashed a pitch off the center field wall that drove Schilling home.

As Geiger pulled into third, the Boston players cheered. Now they were in a 4–4 tie with a runner on third and no one out. But suddenly, to their shocked amazement, they watched Geiger trot jubilantly past third as if he were waiting for their congratulations.

The chowderhead had forgotten the score! He hadn't realized that his hit only tied the game. It didn't win it. Geiger quickly learned his mistake when he was tagged out on a base-running blunder that ultimately cost his team a victory.

"I thought the score was tied when I hit the ball," confessed the chagrined outfielder after the game. "When I ran to third, I saw Schilling score. I thought the winning run was in. Then I heard (third base coach) Billy Herman yelling at me and I turned back. I thought I was going to be congratulated for having knocked in the run. But then I got caught in a rundown and that was it."

The next batter, Carl Yastrzemski, hit what would have been a game-winning sacrifice fly—if it hadn't been for Geiger's boo-boo. The game ended in a tie because of a downpour in the twelfth inning, forcing the entire game to be replayed the next day as part of a doubleheader. The Angels won the makeup game 5–1, much to the dismay of Gary Geiger.

BLIND SPOTS

The Most Flagrantly Blown Calls by Umpires

Umpires are necessary evils, as are batting slumps, bad-hop singles, and cold hot dogs. Without them, what would fans have to complain about? Grudgingly, fans must admit that umpires are pretty honest fellows. It's just that the men in blue aren't always right. You'd swear that some of them worked with a red-tipped cane. For "The Most Flagrantly Blown Calls by Umpires," The Baseball Hall of SHAME inducts the following:

Bill Klem

Sept. 27, 1928

Bill Klem's shocking failure to rule interference on a play that unfolded right before his eyes robbed the New York Giants of a chance at the 1928 pennant.

In the last week of the season, the Giants were only a half game out of first place when they faced the Chicago Cubs. Trailing 3–2 with one out in the sixth inning, New York put runners on second and third.

Batter Shanty Hogan smashed a sharp grounder to pitcher Art Nehf, who wheeled and threw to third baseman Clyde Beck. Andy Reese, the Giant runner on third, charged for the plate, while catcher Gabby Hartnett ran up the line to block Reese. The two collided. Then Hartnett threw his arms around Reese and held him in a bear hug. While Reese wrestled to get free, Beck ran down the line and tagged the runner. Incredibly, Klem ignored the obvious interference and called Reese out.

Within seconds, irate Giants manager John McGraw and his players swarmed around Klem. They hollered and raged. They rightfully charged that Hartnett had interfered, and that Reese should have been allowed to score. But Klem stubbornly refused to listen to reason.

The Giants failed to score in the inning and lost the game, which was played under McGraw's protest. The next day, armed with a *New York Daily News* photograph that clearly showed the interference, McGraw pleaded his case to league president John Heydler. Despite the proof, Heydler upheld Klem. The Giants were crushed; they went on to lose the pennant.

Art Passarella

Oct. 5, 1952

Art Passarella made such a flagrantly bad call in the 1952 World Series that even the commissioner of baseball refused to back him up.

It happened in the bottom of the tenth inning of the fifth game between the Brooklyn Dodgers and the New York Yankees. With the score tied 5–5, Yankee pitcher Johnny Sain hit a slow roller to second baseman Jackie Robinson, who threw late to first. But before the throw even arrived, Passarella called Sain out. Both Sain and coach Bill Dickey argued vehemently, but the umpire stuck by his decision. Buoyed by the unexpected gift, the Dodgers pushed across a run in the top of the eleventh inning and won the game 6–5.

Photos clearly proved Passarella was wrong. When reporters showed commissioner Ford Frick pictures of the disputed call, he declined to come to the umpire's defense. Instead, Frick said, "If I owned a newspaper, I'd blow that picture up to six columns."

That's exactly what *The New York Times* did. The striking photo showed that Sain's left foot had firmly hit the bag while the ball was still several feet away from the outstretched glove of first baseman Gil Hodges.

AP/Wide World Photo

Stump Weidman

June 25–27, 1896

Stump Weidman was the most spineless umpire ever to officiate in the major leagues.

In back-to-back games, he totally lost control of the players and let them walk all over him. They swore at him, threatened him, and shoved him around until the dough-faced umpire was so intimidated that he purposely blew calls to favor the bullies.

Weidman's inexcusable, yellow-bellied umpiring touched off a wild riot that actually led to the arrest of the tormenting team.

This incredible story of arbiter shame began on June 25, 1896, in a game Weidman was officiating between the gentlemanly Louisville Colonels and the visiting Cleveland Spiders, one of the rowdiest teams in the National League.

In the third inning, the Spiders (who later won 8–3) crowded the umpire and argued over a close call. Outfielder Jesse Burkett was furious. He grabbed Weidman by the shoulders and shook him the way a cat shakes a rat. Another Cleveland player bowled into the ump. The crowd raged in protest, but Weidman meekly took the indignities—and just brushed off his clothes.

The wimpy umpire was so afraid of Spider player-manager Patsy Tebeau and his men that he deliberately made bad calls against the Colonels in the game the following day.

"It was possibly the worst attempt at umpiring that was ever made on a National League diamond," declared the *Louisville Courier-Journal*. The account added, "Mr. Weidman has no more business umpiring a game of ball than a six-year-old boy. Time and again he tried to rob the Louisvilles of the victory they had fairly won, evidently in great fear of the Spiders, who had shaken his teeth loose the day before. Both teams made a sorry spectacle of Mr. Weidman, and if he was not willing to resign last night, his endurance and forbearance are more than human. The umpire had been pulled and hauled around like a straw man which no one had any especial use for but to kick and cuff about."

Realizing that Weidman could not control the Spiders, Louisville manager Bill McGunnigle ordered his genteel team to be as belligerent and rough as Cleveland. The Colonels entered into the spirit of this decision with considerable zeal and argued with Weidman on most every call.

In the first inning the Colonels had every right to protest. Weidman robbed Louisville of two hits by declaring Tom McCreery and Charlie Dexter out after both had clearly beaten throws to first base. On balls and strikes, the umpire gave Louisville the worst of it, causing the Colonels to scream in outrage and threaten him with bodily harm.

Occasionally, he knuckled under to their bullying and made a call to their liking. But that just brought on the wrath of the Spiders.

According to the account in the *Courier-Journal*, "When [Weidman] failed to give everything to Cleveland, Tebeau and his Spiders would run at him like mad bulls. 'Just wait, I'll get you!' 'You'll never be umpiring by the Fourth of July!'

"Many vile epithets were used by the Spiders. They called the umpire everything they could think of, and in this line they think rapidly. It was a pity that so many women were in the grandstand to witness such rowdy- ism and to hear the epithets the Spiders used.

"Louisville won the game at least three times had Umpire Weidman given the home team half a chance."

As darkness descended on the field at the end of the ninth inning, the score was tied 4–4, and the Colonels asked Weidman to call the game. The umpire turned to Spiders manager Tebeau, who yelled, "No!" So Weidman announced, "Play ball!"

In the tenth inning, the Colonels tried stalling to force the umpire to call the game. They dallied after grounders, threw the ball away, and dropped pop-ups. After the Spiders had scored three runs, they tried to speed the game up by hitting easy grounders, but the Colonels refused to throw them out. So the Spiders deliberately struck out to retire the side.

The game at this point was a howling farce. Fans were yelling that they couldn't see the ball and begging the umpire to call the game, a decision which would have reverted the score to the way it was at the end of the ninth inning. Again, Tebeau looked at Weidman and shouted, "No!" So the umpire compliantly said, "Play ball!"

In the bottom of the tenth, the Colonels stalled; the batters took their time picking imaginary bugs off their trousers. By now it was so dark that Spiders pitcher Nig Cuppy could hardly see the plate, and he walked the bases loaded.

"Oh, it's too dark to see the ball," said the umpire. "I call the game." He started to walk toward the players' bench while the Colonels whooped happily and kicked up their heels.

The angry Spiders swarmed around Weidman in protest, and outfielder Jimmy McAleer belted him. The blow was like a signal to riot and hun- dreds of fans leaped from the stands.

Before the police arrived, Weidman was pummeled by several Spiders, who, in turn, were being beaten by the fans. The cops finally broke up the fracas and escorted the Spiders to their omnibus while the crowd jeered and threw rocks. Said the *Courier-Journal*, "It was a pathetic sight to see half the brave Cleveland team, lying stomachs down, in the bottom of the omnibus, dodging flying brickbats and boulders."

The next day, Saturday, June 27, while the teams were at the ball park waiting for the rain to stop, eight Spiders were arrested and hauled before

Louisville's Judge Thompson. He found four guilty of breaching the peace and fined Tebeau $100, Ed McKean and Jimmy McAleer $75 each, and Jesse Burkett $50. The judge dropped the charges against the rest of the players.

As the Spiders left to a hissing crowd, Tebeau shouted, "Even Steven! Wait until youse gets to Cleveland!"

Bill Stewart

Oct. 6, 1948

National League umpire Bill Stewart was caught flat-footed on a crucial pickoff play—and he cost the Cleveland Indians the opening game of the 1948 World Series.

Before facing the Boston Braves in the Series opener, Indians player-manager Lou Boudreau alerted the umpiring crew to watch out for his team's timed pickoff play, which had worked successfully eight times during the year. In the umpire's dressing room, Stewart dismissed the warning and boasted to his fellow arbiters that he had never been caught off guard by a pickoff play. Unfortunately, he would a few hours later.

Cleveland's Bob Feller and Boston's Johnny Sain hurled shutouts until the bottom of the eighth inning, when the Braves had runners Phil Masi at second and Sibby Sisti on first.

With two out and Tommy Holmes at bat, shortstop Lou Boudreau hovered at second to keep Masi close. But Masi, representing the winning run, edged off the bag anyway. Then Boudreau touched his knee to signal the pickoff play. All the umpires knew what was about to happen. Except Stewart.

On a prearranged count, Feller wheeled and fired to second. Boudreau, who timed the play perfectly, darted over to the bag, speared the ball, and slapped it on Masi who was diving desperately back to the base. The pickoff had worked. Everyone—players, fans, and photographers—knew that Masi was nailed for the third out of the inning. But a startled Stewart blindly called Masi safe.

Boudreau protested vigorously, but to no avail. Moments later, Holmes lashed a single and Masi—granted a reprieve by Stewart—streaked around third and crossed the plate with the game's only run. A tainted run.

THE ONES WHO GOT AWAY

Teams That Foolishly Failed to Hold on to Future Superstars

Unlike fishermen, baseball owners don't like to talk about the big ones that got away. Future sluggers and pitching stars have been hooked and then tossed away or allowed to wriggle free because some bait-brain in the front office couldn't recognize a prize catch if it jumped up and bit him. For "Teams That Foolishly Failed to Hold On to Future Superstars," The Baseball Hall of SHAME inducts the following:

Pirates' Loss of Walter Johnson

1907

All that stood in the way of putting Walter Johnson in a Pirate's uniform was some cheapskate in the front office. Johnson was attracting a lot of attention around the ball parks of the Pacific Northwest with his blazing fastball.

Stunned by the kid's speed and control, a friend of Pittsburgh manager Fred Clarke urged the skipper to bring the pitching sensation back east for a tryout. All Johnson needed was a nine dollar advance for his train fare. Nope, said the front office. No advance for some unknown.

Walter Johnson missed that train ride. But he eventually took another trip, to Washington, D.C., and stayed 21 years, collecting an unparalleled 416 career victories in the American League.

Red Sox' Loss of Jackie Robinson

1944

The Boston Red Sox muffed a once-in-a-lifetime opportunity to make history—and in a way that would have strengthened the team. They had first crack at signing Jackie Robinson but, blinded by prejudice, they turned him down flat.

To pacify local civil rights leaders, the Red Sox gave a short tryout to three Negro League stars, including Robinson, a gifted athlete from the Kansas City Monarchs. Robinson impressed Boston manager Joe Cronin with his dazzling fielding and hitting. But management told Jackie that it was against team policy to sign players after so short a tryout. He was given the "don't call us, we'll call you" routine.

The truth was that Boston did not want blacks on its team. In fact, it was not until 15 years later, in 1959, that the Red Sox finally integrated—the last team to do so—when it signed Pumpsie Green.

Instead of making history with the Boston Red Sox, Robinson broke the color barrier with the Brooklyn Dodgers in 1947. In his freshman year in the majors, Robinson led the Dodgers to the pennant and earned baseball's first Rookie of the Year award.

More importantly, Jackie Robinson opened the door for other blacks to play in the bigs.

Reds' Loss of Babe Ruth

1914

If scout Harry Stevens had known anything about baseball, Babe Ruth would have started his major league career with the Cincinnati Reds.

In 1914, Ruth was playing for the Baltimore Orioles of the International League. The team had an agreement that allowed the Reds to purchase any two players from the Orioles' roster. The task of signing the pair of prospects was handed to Stevens—a flunky with no baseball savvy. The only reason he had a scouting job was because he was a close friend of the Fleischmann family, owners of the Reds.

Stevens watched a few games in Baltimore and made his decision—a terribly bad one. He failed to see the enormous potential of Ruth, and rejected the power-hitting pitcher. Instead, Stevens chose Claud Derrick, who lasted two games with the Reds, and George Twombly, who batted a paltry .221 over the next three years.

Meanwhile, Ruth went on to become the greatest player the game has ever seen—but not as a member of the Cincinnati Reds.

It's unclear whether Stevens remained a friend of the Fleischmann family.

Mets' Loss of Reggie Jackson

1966

The amateur free agent draft is, admittedly, a chancy thing. But it can also be an untapped gold mine.

In 1966, the Mets had the first pick in the draft of high school and college players. They took some kid named Steve Chilcott. They passed over a collegiate star named Reggie Jackson.

Unable to believe their good fortune, the Kansas City A's grabbed the young slugger, who had been marked for superstardom by almost every major league scout. Jackson became one of the game's great personalities, an All-Star, the 1973 American League MVP, and a three-time home run champ.

Steve Chilcott never made it to the bigs.

Cubs' Loss of Joe DiMaggio

1935

During the winter of 1935, Chicago Cubs owner William Wrigley was given a "can't lose" offer. Yet, in his own inimitable way, Wrigley managed to lose.

The deal was proposed by Charles Graham, owner of the San Francisco Seals of the Pacific Coast League. He tried to sell his young center fielder, Joe DiMaggio, to Wrigley for $25,000. But Wrigley was wary of a knee injury that DiMaggio had suffered the year before.

To allay any fears, Graham told Wrigley to take DiMaggio on a trial basis, and that if the owner wasn't satisfied after a thorough looking-over, Graham would take DiMaggio back and return the purchase price.

Despite this generous, no-risk, money-back guarantee, Wrigley still shook his head no. The next year, Cub fans shook their heads in dismay when DiMaggio tore up the American League with his hitting and launched a Hall of Fame career with the Yankees.

Dodgers' Loss of George Kell

1942

The initial scouting report on George Kell sounded as if it came from some tout at the track talking about a nag headed for the glue factory: "Too fat ... bad leg."

Larry MacPhail, president of the Dodgers, dropped by spring training camp to find out what baseball players did to earn their keep. At the time, Kell, a rookie third baseman, was limping from an injury, and looked a little overweight to MacPhail.

"I'm tired of feeding kids who aren't going anyplace," MacPhail grumped. He ordered his staff to dump Kell.

The Philadelphia Athletics gladly picked up Kell, who showed he could vacuum-clean any grounder hit to third and knock the hide off the ball.

Kell was a thoroughbred winner who played 15 years in the majors and finished with a lifetime .306 batting average.

Tigers' Loss of Carl Hubbell

1926

When he was the manager of the Detroit Tigers, Ty Cobb let Carl Hubbell slip through his fingers. And it was all because of Hubbell's screwball—the pitch that the hurler would later throw to win 24 consecutive games.

When Hubbell was trying to make the team during spring training in 1926, Cobb ordered him not to throw the screwball because Cobb thought it would ruin the young pitcher's arm. Deprived of his best pitch, Hubbell floundered on the mound, and the Tigers eventually gave him an unconditional release.

Hubbell then signed with a minor league team that let him throw his screwball. Flinging his favorite pitch, Hubbell baffled batters and impressed the New York Giants enough for them to buy him for $25,000. "King Carl" went on to win 253 games in 16 years with the Giants and was voted into the Hall of Fame.

TAKE ME OUT TO THE BRAWL GAME

The Most Flagrant Cases of Assault and Battery on the Field

Baseball players can hit, but few can fight. A typical fracas between teams looks like a 50-percent-off sale at Macy's—lots of shoving, a little scuffling, and some harsh words. But every now and then, the baseball field takes on the ugly specter of street-gang warfare. Players wield bats to bash heads, not baseballs. They throw punches rather than pitches. For "The Most Flagrant Cases of Assault and Battery on the Field," The Baseball Hall of SHAME inducts the following:

New York Yankees vs. Washington Senators

First Bout: Washington • July 4, 1932
Rematch: Washington • April 25, 1933

A devastating and needless one-punch fight sparked a blood feud that wasn't settled until the following season in one of the wildest baseball riots of the century.

In the first bout, fistic fireworks erupted during the opening game of a doubleheader between the Yankees and the Senators at Griffith Stadium. On a close play at the plate in the seventh inning, Washington's Carl Reynolds plowed into catcher Bill Dickey and knocked the ball loose. The impact sent Dickey tumbling.

Bellowing like a wounded bull, Dickey came off the ground and, without warning, threw a looping right-handed punch. The blow caught Reynolds flat-footed and shattered his jaw in two places. Players charged out of the dugouts to do battle, but no one else was hurt.

Reynolds and Dickey were kicked out of the game. American League president William Harridge fined Dickey $1,000 and suspended him for the nearly six weeks that Reynolds had to sit out while recovering from the jaw breaker.

The winter didn't cool tempers in Washington. The next season, in the first series between the two clubs, war broke out. Yankees fought Senators, players fought fans, cops fought players and fans, and umpires fought players, fans, and cops.

The tumult ignited in the fourth inning, when Yankee Ben Chapman broke up a double play by spiking second baseman Buddy Myer. To get even, Myer kicked Chapman, and the two came to blows. With the Washington fans howling, both teams poured onto the field for the obligatory pushing and shoving match. Despite all the bad blood, however, cooler heads prevailed, and the game continued without Chapman and Myer, who were ejected from the game.

To get to the Yankee clubhouse, Chapman had to pass the Washington dugout, where he heard pitcher Earl Whitehill utter a few choice comments about Chapman's playing and fighting abilities. Chapman responded by socking Whitehill in the jaw—not too smart considering that the Yankee was surrounded by Senators, who proceeded to pummel him to the floor.

Seeing his buddy go down in enemy territory, Dixie Walker rushed to his rescue—along with most of the rest of the Yankees. Then hundreds of fans streamed from the stands and leaped into the fray. Out in the right field bleachers, some foolhardy Yankee fans announced their loyalties and were promptly pounced on by a mob of angry Washingtonians.

Meanwhile, back at the main event, a police riot squad, swinging nightsticks, charged into the fist-flying maelstrom. Instead of herding the fans off the field, the cops assaulted the Yankees. One officer rushed into the dugout, flashed his badge, and declared, "I'll take charge of this!" He socked Chapman, but then disappeared under a mass of pinstripes.

Another cop was whomping New York pitcher Lefty Gomez with a blackjack when teammate Don Brennan came to Gomez's aid. In the confusion, Gomez decked his fellow Yankee by mistake.

The biggest guy on the field, New York pitcher Jumbo Brown, made one cop pay the price for messing with the Yankees. In a fight with the bluecoat, Brown came out wearing the policeman's helmet and badge.

When not battling cops, the Yankees fought with fans. New York manager Joe McCarthy was knocked on his butt while arguing with a fastidious old man wearing a pince-nez. Another rabble-rouser grabbed a bat and charged after Chapman, but his teammates tackled the attacker and stomped on him.

Nearby, umpires George Moriarty and Harry Geisel began indiscriminately heaving Yankees, Senators, fans, and cops out of the way in a determined effort to quell the rampage. Before order was finally restored, Yankee pitcher Johnny Allen chased Senators infielder John Kerr all over the field after Kerr berated him with insults.

Through it all, two Yankee greats remained firmly planted in their dugout, laughing at the bedlam—Babe Ruth and Lou Gehrig.

Eventually, the players returned to their positions, the fans climbed back into the stands, and the police headed for the station with five troublemakers in tow.

After defending the home team with their fists, the fans quickly turned on the Senators and booed them throughout the rest of the game as the Yankees won in a rout, 16–0.

Umpire George Moriarty vs. Chicago White Sox

Cleveland • May 30, 1932

In the most violent clash between an umpire and players in modern baseball history, George Moriarty duked it out with four pugnacious members of the Chicago White Sox.

It was a split decision.

Tempers were frayed throughout the Memorial Day doubleheader in Cleveland as the White Sox questioned Moriarty's eyesight and ancestry much of the afternoon. It reached a feverish pitch in the bottom of the ninth inning of the second game, with the White Sox ahead 11–9.

The Indians rallied and had the winning runs on base when Milt Gaston fired a 2–2 pitch to Earl Averill. Gaston thought it was strike three but Moriarty, umpiring behind the plate, called ball three. Averill belted the next pitch for a game-winning triple.

AP/Wide World Photo

As the ump headed for the dressing room, the White Sox heckled and cursed him. Fearing for his safety, several Indians crowded around Moriarty and urged him to hurry before trouble broke out. "Don't try to rush me, boys. I'm not afraid of what these fellows will do," said the hard-as-nails, six-foot, 200-pound arbiter.

In the runway leading to the clubhouse, Chicago catcher Charlie Berry, a former football All-American, challenged the umpire to a fight. "I'll take on the whole White Sox club!" bellowed Moriarty. "I'll fight all of you one at a time."

Gaston threw down his glove and stepped forward. "You might as well start with me." So Moriarty did. He floored the pitcher with a solid right to the jaw.

White Sox manager Lew Fonseca, Berry, and another catcher, Frank Grube, also a former college football star, then piled onto the 47-year-old umpire. As Moriarty tumbled to the floor, the White Sox pummeled him and kicked him in the head. Several Indians tried to pull them off him, but Moriarty was so tough that he still got in his licks and shouted at his rescuers, "Don't interfere!" But they did anyway.

Moriarty was taken to the hospital and treated for a broken hand (from knocking out Gaston), spike wounds to his head, and bruises to his face.

Fonseca immediately claimed that Moriarty went out of his way to invite trouble: "The tipoff is that he left the field through the players' runway toward the clubhouse instead of going to the umpire's dressing room by the usual route. He spent the afternoon begging for trouble—and he finally got it."

American League president Will Harridge scoffed at Fonseca's weak excuse, fined all four White Sox, and suspended Gaston for 10 days.

It was the only time that Moriarty was the loser in a brawl—and it had taken three opponents to get him down. The White Sox had forgotten what a bruiser he was. Once, during his days as a third baseman for the Detroit Tigers, he had argued with the mean, feared Ty Cobb. As they readied for fisticuffs, Moriarty handed Cobb a bat and said, "This makes it even." Then he proceeded to beat the pit out of the Georgia Peach.

Cincinnati Reds vs. New York Mets and Fans

New York • Oct. 8, 1973

Fists, beer cans, and even whiskey bottles flew through the clamorous air at Shea Stadium as the Cincinnati Reds fought the New York Mets and their fans in the most deplorable play-off fracas ever.

And it was all touched off by none other than Cincy star Pete Rose.

In the fifth inning of the third game of the National League Championship Series, the Mets were blowing out the Reds 9–2. That's when Rose let his frustrations warp his judgment. Out on a force play at second base, Rose angrily and deliberately barreled into little Bud Harrelson. The 192-pound Rose pushed and shoved the 146-pound shortstop and then the two wrestled in the dirt. Players on both sides spilled out of the dugouts and bull pens to join in a wild-swinging melee that also featured a toe-to-toe slugfest between Mets pitcher Buzz Capra and Reds pitcher Pedro Borbon.

Eventually, the players separated and the dust settled. However, the 53,967 Metsomaniacs remained inflamed when the Reds took the field. A beer can struck Reds pitcher Gary Nolan in the bull pen. But the main target was Rose in left field. Rabid fans flung not only threats but also garbage at the fiery troublemaker. Rose responded in kind, hurling the junk back at them. After a beer can hit him and a whiskey bottle whizzed by his ear, Rose sought shelter in the dugout, and manager Sparky Anderson ordered all his troops off the field.

The Reds' withdrawal did nothing to calm the crowd, which became further provoked by Borbon. After his fight with Capra, Borbon discovered he had somehow ended up wearing a hated Mets cap. So, in a gesture for all to see, Borbon bit the cap and ripped it apart. The fans screamed in outrage.

Finally, National League president Chub Feeney walked out onto the field and warned the Mets that he would forfeit the game to the Reds unless the disorderly crowd in left field was brought under control. To negotiate a truce, the Mets appointed a peace commission of Willie Mays, Yogi Berra, Tom Seaver, Cleon Jones, and Rusty Staub.

The delegation stood in no-man's-land in left field where Willie, with outstretched arms, appealed for calm. The peace mission proved successful, and the delegation marched triumphantly back to the dugout while

New York Times Pictures

nine attendants cleared the field of debris. The game continued, and the Mets finished what they had started, a 9–2 drubbing of the Reds.

A far from repentant Rose added a postscript to the trashing of Shea and the assault on Harrelson when he declared, "I'll be honest. I was trying to knock him into left field."

Ruben Gomez vs. Joe Adcock

Milwaukee • July 17, 1955

This could have been a fun fight. But Ruben Gomez brought shame to generations of basebrawlers. He ran.

In the bottom of the second inning, the New York Giants pitcher hit Milwaukee Braves first baseman Joe Adcock on the wrist with a brushback pitch. Boiling mad, the Braves first baseman gestured belligerently as he headed for first. After swapping invectives, Adcock, a hulking 6-foot, 4-inch, 210 pounder, stalked toward 6-foot, 170-pound Gomez. When the two were 20 feet apart, the frightened hurler fired a bullet that hit Adcock again, this time on the left thigh.

Usually these incidents result in a fight on the mound. But not this one. With lightning in his eyes and thunder in his fists, Adcock rushed at Gomez, who hightailed it toward the dugout at jackrabbit speed. Third base coach Johnny Riddle tried to flag down the flying Gomez with a tackle, but missed. The pitcher scurried into the safety of the Giants clubhouse as his teammates closed ranks and waited for the onrushing Adcock and the rest of the Braves.

Several minor skirmishes broke out among the players, who paid no attention when the stadium organist played the national anthem. After order finally was restored, both Gomez and Adcock were tossed out of the game.

Gomez, in the protective custody of three Milwaukee plainclothesmen, sat in the Giant clubhouse in street clothes and faced the writers. "He charged me so I threw the ball at him again," said the Puerto Rican-born hurler. "I didn't miss either. I don't let him break my ribs." Five detectives provided Gomez safe escort to his hotel.

Players on both teams were upset, not because Gomez had deliberately thrown at Adcock to hurt him, but that the pitcher didn't stand and fight.

"It was disgraceful, his running," said one teammate. Even Gomez's manager, Bill Rigney, felt the same way. "I'm sorry he ran," Rigney said. "I'd have been out there soon enough to save him from a beating."

National League president Warren Giles suspended Gomez for three days and fined him $200, while Adcock was fined $100.

More than ten years later, Giles revealed a shocking postscript to this sorry incident. Giles admitted to reporters that after Gomez's panic-stricken flight into the clubhouse, the pitcher had grabbed a knife and returned to the dugout to meet Adcock.

"It could have been really serious," said Giles. "We hushed it up at the time as the situation was bad enough without bringing the knife into it."

Manager Birdie Tebbetts vs. Manager Harry Walker

Cincinnati • July 5, 1955

As leaders of men, managers must set examples for their young charges by remaining cool in close, tense ball games. But Cincinnati Reds pilot Birdie Tebbetts and St. Louis Cardinals field boss Harry Walker lost their heads.

In the sort of fight seldom, if ever, seen in modern baseball, both managers battled in the dirt like a couple of junkyard dogs. Fans weren't the only ones stunned. So was National League president Warren Giles, who watched the shameful scrap from the grandstand.

The Reds posed a threat with two out in the bottom of the ninth inning of a 4–4 tie when Walker brought in pitcher Paul LaPalme. After Walker returned to the dugout, catcher Bill Sarni lingered on the mound to talk with his pitcher. Their conversation dragged on and on.

Finally, Tebbetts ran out to home-plate umpire Jocko Conlon and complained that the Cards were stalling. He threatened to protest the game. Conlon went out to the mound and warned LaPalme and Sarni that he'd start calling balls whether any had been thrown or not.

Then Walker charged out of the dugout and started jawing with Tebbetts at home plate. Walker claimed his players had every right to take their time. The two managers traded names—and then punches. In seconds, they were rolling on the ground, snarling and wrestling, while players from both sides joined the fight.

Stadium cops rushed out and restored order, but not before Ted Kluszewski, Cincy's 230-pound first baseman, grabbed 160-pound Cards infielder Solly Hemus with one hand, holding off two other St. Louis players with his other hand.

Tebbetts, who admitted throwing the first punch, was bleeding from the mouth when it was over, but he stuck around to see his Reds score the winning run a few minutes later.

The next day, Giles called the managers' fist fight "unprecedented" in baseball, and fined them each $100. "Managers have an obligation to preserve and restore order," said Giles, "and not by their own actions incite disorder."

Dixie Walker vs. Len Merullo

Brooklyn • May 1, 1946

It was the most shameful, fiercest brawl ever to take place *before* a game started.

Twenty-five city police rushed to Ebbets Field to prevent a fan riot when players formed a ring around the knock-down-drag-out slugfest between Chicago Cubs shortstop Len Merullo and Brooklyn Dodgers outfielder Dixie Walker. While their bare fists cracked into flesh and bone, Merullo and Walker were surrounded by a seething bedlam of pathos, heated action, and comedy.

Walker's 9-year-old son, Fred Jr., leaped out of the stands crying, "Daddy! Daddy!" but couldn't crash the determined ring around his fighting father. A burly park cop broke into the ring, but Cubs catcher Clyde McCullough picked him up and tossed him out. When police reinforcements arrived, Cub teammates Bill Nicholson and Billy Jurges tangled with the Brooklyn gendarmes until threatened with arrest. The players were saved by their manager Charlie Grimm, who barked to the cops, "Don't you dare lay a hand on my boys!"

The unprecedented fisticuffs erupted during Dodger batting practice an hour before game time. Merullo walked over to Pee Wee Reese and accused the Dodger shortstop of hitting him from behind in a scuffle at second base in the previous day's game. Merullo called Reese an uncomplimentary name and added, "And that goes for your whole damn ball club too."

With that, Dixie Walker punched Merullo on the side of the head. To avoid a two-team free-for-all, brawny Cubs pitcher Paul Erickson separated Walker and Merullo and ordered the other players to form a ring around the two combatants so they could fight it out for themselves.

Merullo and Walker kicked, gouged, and slugged each other for about eight minutes, and quit only when their bodies were more bruised than their pride.

The partisan Brooklyn crowd's shouts diminished when they saw that their favorite, Walker, had lost the decision. Walker, his shirt tattered and soiled from blood and dirt, had lost one tooth and broken another. Merullo suffered a baseball-sized lump behind his ear. To prevent a rematch, police remained in both dugouts throughout the game, won by Brooklyn, 2–1. Both players were fined and suspended the next day.

So where was Reese, one of the principals in triggering the fight? He later revealed, "Since they started the fight over me, I thought I ought to make a showing, so I began inching towards Stanky. But [the Cubs'] Phil Cavarretta sat on me, so I just lay there peacefully."

BUBBLE GUM BOZOS

The Most Unprofessional Baseball Cards

Somewhere in those stacks of baseball cards there's a card to suit every taste—poor taste, that is. The bubbleheaded poses some players have gotten away with should be in a rogues' gallery instead of a bubble gum card collection. And the companies who deal these cards have been caught in more than one fast shuffle themselves. For "The Most Unprofessional Baseball Cards," The Baseball Hall of SHAME inducts the following:

Claude Raymond

Pitcher • Houston, N.L. • 1966–67

Claude Raymond had trouble with flies. Not the kind you catch or swat; the kind you zipper. For Topps card number 586 in 1966, he struck a very revealing pose—his fly was open.

In true Hall of Shame style, Raymond exposed himself to further ridicule the following year, when Topps card number 364 featured him again with an unzipped fly.

Tommy John

Pitcher • Chicago, A.L. • 1969

Though known as a smart pitcher, Tommy John didn't look too bright on his baseball card. When he was being photographed for Topps card number 465, John chose the classic hurler's pose. He followed through on his pitching motion as if he had just thrown a high hard one.

There was one embarrassing problem. He forgot that the ball was still nestled securely in the center of his glove for all to see.

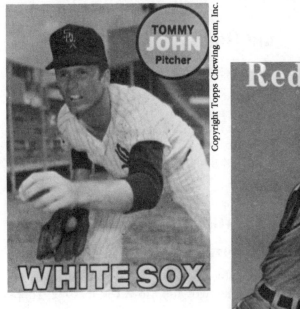

Topps Chewing Gum Co.

1958

An overzealous Topps artist made Detroit catcher Red Wilson look like baseball's answer to the Venus de Milo. In 1958, the card company painted out the natural background of the photos.

But the artist went too far on Topps card number 213, and painted out the bat that Wilson was swinging. As a result, Wilson, who was following through on his swing, strikes a shamefully disarming pose.

Fleer Corp.

1982

Fleer attempted to honor perfection, but struck out instead. In 1982, it issued card number 639 featuring Cleveland Indians hurler Len Barker's perfect game of May 15, 1981. On the front, the card shows Barker with catcher Bo Diaz, and on the back it lauds the two battery mates.

In reality, Bo Diaz did not catch Barker's historic game. Unheralded teammate Ron Hassey was the one calling the right pitches behind the plate. But Hassey was neither pictured nor credited on the card.

Joe Hoerner

Pitcher • Philadelphia, N.L. • 1976

For his photograph on SSPC's card number 456, Joe Hoerner traded his baseball cap for a silly sunbonnet and pensively rested his chin on his hand. He looked like he belonged in the bush leagues, not the big leagues.

History proved his pose was quite appropriate. After the card came out, he didn't win another major league game in two years of trying, and finally quit baseball.

Topps Chewing Gum Co.

1972

Kids want to know as much as possible about their favorite players, so the back of each Topps card crams in plenty of info. However, in 1972, Topps overdid things on Sparky Lyle's card.

A question-and-answer feature on the back of card number 259 appeared to give kids an intimate (and presumably erroneous) glimpse at the sex life of the Boston Red Sox pitcher. The question, as it appeared on Lyle's card, asked, "How long is the pitcher's rubber?" Imagine what wide-eyed adolescents must have thought of Lyle when they looked at the answer: "24 inches."

Gary Pettis

Outfielder • California, A.L. • 1985

Topps says card number 497 is that of Angels outfielder Gary Pettis. But that's no Angel on the card.

Taking advantage of the fact that he wasn't a household name, Pettis pulled a devilish trick on the card company and let a teenager impersonate him. The phony in the Angels uniform is really Pettis's 16-year-old brother, Lynn.

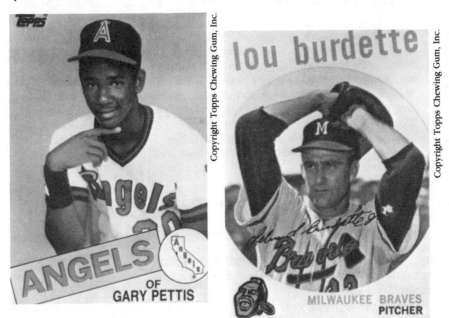

Lew Burdette

Pitcher • Milwaukee, N.L. • 1959

There's a joker dealt every spring when players are photographed for baseball cards. Burdette was it in 1959.

For Topps card number 440, the right-handed, 20-game winner posed as a lefthander. Burdette added an extra touch to further insult the intelligence of the fans. The card shows him at the top of his windup ready to throw a pitch—except there is no ball, only a fist clenching thin air.

The Topps people were embarrassed because Burdette sneaked one over on them. But they had another reason to feel foolish. They misspelled his first name. The card reads "Lou" when it should read "Lew."

WELCOME TO THE BIGS!

The Most Inauspicious Major League Debuts

Aspiring major leaguers dream about what that glorious first day in the bigs will be like. They see themselves hammering the winning homer with two out in the bottom of the ninth, or leaping high against the fence to make a game-saving catch. That's the fantasy. The reality is that in their diamond debuts they often stumble over their feet, fall flat on their faces, or otherwise disgrace themselves so badly that they carry a stigma with them the rest of their careers—which can be a whole lot shorter than they'd planned. For "The Most Inauspicious Major League Debuts," The Baseball Hall of SHAME inducts the following:

Joe Nuxhall

Pitcher • Cincinnati, N.L. • June 10, 1944

Joe Nuxhall was so rattled when told to warm up for his first major league game that he tripped over the dugout steps and fell flat on his kisser. It was an ominous sign of things to come.

During the wartime year of 1944, when teams short of manpower were looking under rocks for playing talent, the Cincinnati Reds signed Nuxhall, a 15-year-old ninth grader. Since he was still in school, Nuxhall joined the team on weekends and for a few night games during the week.

On a Saturday afternoon in Crosley Field, the St. Louis Cardinals were creaming the Reds 13–0. Nuxhall was sitting on the bench in utter fascination because he had seen so few big league games. Suddenly, his reverie was interrupted by manager Bill McKechnie, who said, "Go to the bull pen, Joe, and warm up."

The unexpectedness of an assignment so soon after signing a contract paralyzed Nuxhall's nerves. He had had no idea he'd get to pitch. He tripped and landed on his face as he headed for the bull pen. The nervous and shaken teenager fired several wild balls during his warm-up. But ready or not, the boy took the mound to start the ninth inning, becoming the youngest player ever to appear in the majors.

Nuxhall had walked two and had recorded two outs when he came face to face with Stan Musial, the previous year's batting champion. Musial ripped a run-scoring single. For a boy who had been pitching against junior high school kids just a few weeks earlier, the pressure was too much to handle. Nuxhall lost his composure. He proceeded to give up five runs, five walks, two wild pitches, and two hits in two-thirds of an inning before McKechnie mercifully took Nuxhall out of the game.

Two days later, Nuxhall was on a train for Birmingham, Alabama, the home of Cincy's farm team in the lowly Sally League.

It was eight years before Nuxhall returned to the majors and recorded his third big league out.

Doe Boyland

First baseman • Pittsburgh, N. L. • Sept. 4, 1978

In his first major league at-bat, Pirates rookie Doe Boyland struck out— while sitting on the bench.

In the seventh inning of a home game against the Mets, manager Chuck Tanner sent Boyland in to pinch-hit for pitcher Ed Whitson. The count was one ball and two strikes when Mets right-handed pitcher Skip Lockwood had to leave the game because he'd hurt his arm.

The Mets switched to southpaw Kevin Kobel, so Tanner, going by the book, lifted the left-handed swinging Boyland and put in right-handed hitter Rennie Stennett to pinch-hit for the pinchhitter.

While Boyland watched with dismay from the bench, Stennett struck out on Kobel's first pitch. Under the scoring rules, the strikeout was charged to Boyland.

Frank Verdi

Shortstop • New York, A.L. • May 10, 1953

Frank Verdi said his first at-bat in the major leagues was "like your first date—it's something you can never forget." Only in his case, it was like getting stood up.

After languishing in the Yankees' farm system for seven years, Verdi finally made the big club. He sat on the bench until that fateful Sunday in Boston's Fenway Park when he filled in at shortstop for Phil Rizzuto, who had been taken out in the sixth inning for a pinchhitter.

In the top of the seventh, Verdi was all set to make his long-awaited debut at the plate. The Yankees had rallied to take a two-run lead and had the bases loaded with two out. What a great moment for Verdi. All the years of toiling in the minors—the sweaty bus rides, the two-bit towns, the fleabag hotels—were about to pay off. Here was his golden opportunity to knock in some important runs in his first big league at-bat.

Verdi stepped into the batter's box, anxious to hit. But then he heard Red Sox coach Bill McKechnie shout, "Time out!" McKechnie sent pitcher Ellis Kinder to the showers and brought in reliever Ken Holcombe. After the new pitcher completed his warm-up tosses, Verdi stepped back into the batter's box.

Once again, he heard, "Time out!" This time it was Yankee manager Casey Stengel. Verdi turned around and saw teammate Bill Renna swinging three bats. Stengel was sending him up to pinch-hit for Verdi. That was Verdi's debut in the bigs. It was also his finale. He was sent back to the minors, never to return.

"At least," he said, "I got in the batter's box twice. A lot of guys only got in once."

Texas Rangers' Food Ban

April 3, 1984

When a new policy prohibiting spectators from bringing food and drinks into Arlington Stadium made its debut, it left a bad taste in the mouths of Texas Rangers fans.

Not content to simply make money on tickets and parking, the Rangers management made fans buy their food in the stadium or go hungry.

Although the club announced before Opening Day that it would no longer allow families to bring their picnic goodies into the stadium, some fans dared to defy the ban. They brought food and drinks to the game, as they had been doing for 12 years. This time, however, they were stopped and frisked at the gate.

One spectator had his sack of sandwiches impounded at the turnstile. When he went back to retrieve it after the game, he was handed his sack—which now contained only one sandwich and three empty wrappers.

At least he was given *some* food back. Not so lucky was fan Tom Thompson, who brought fried chicken to eat at the game. The ever-vigilant food confiscators at the gate took his finger-lickin'-good contraband away from him. Thompson went to the stadium manager to protest the new policy, but was even angrier when he returned to the gate. "I went to complain," Thompson said, "and when I got back, they were eating my chicken."

When told of the incident by reporters, a Rangers official tried to laugh it off by joking, "We told them (security guards) that the job didn't pay much, but they get all the food they can eat."

Because of the ban, the concession stands were overburdened, resulting in long lines of irate fans who complained they missed whole innings of the game. (That was probably a blessing in disguise, since the Rangers were blown out by the Cleveland Indians 9–1.)

Since the food ban struck out so badly in its debut, club officials eventually benched it and reinstated the old policy.

Lou Stringer

Shortstop • Chicago, N.L. • April 14, 1941

Chicago Cubs rookie Lou Stringer grabbed all the headlines in his major league debut. He even put himself in the record book—by committing the most errors (four) of any shortstop on Opening Day.

There was no doubt Stringer was nervous. When the Cubs streaked out of their Wrigley Field dugout to take their positions for the first inning of the year, he forgot to bring his glove! Sheepishly, he ran back to get it.

The glove didn't do him much good. In the first inning, Stringer bobbled Pirate Arky Vaughan's grounder and threw wildly to first for an error. In the second inning, Stringer let Al Lopez's grounder skip between his legs.

Stringer didn't do any more fielding damage until the ninth inning, when he must have wanted to add some excitement to the game. Although the Cubs entered the inning with a 7–2 lead, the shaky shortstop made a wild throw and booted an apparent game-ending double-play ball to give the Pirates a chance to win. Pittsburgh, with only one out, had the bases loaded and the potential winning run at the plate. But the Cubs survived, 7–4, no thanks to Stringer's dubious debut.

Cal Browning

Pitcher • St. Louis, N. L. • June 12, 1960

Cal Browning's heart was thumping. Just days ago, he was in the minors, pitching for Rochester. Now, clad in a St. Louis Cardinals uniform, he was about to play in his very first major league game.

Browning had gone to the mound in relief of veteran Ron Kline. The 22-year-old rookie was already sweating, not from the humid St. Louis heat, but from sheer nervousness.

Into the batter's box stepped crafty hitter Don Hoak, third baseman for the Pittsburgh Pirates. As he finished his warm-up tosses, Browning remembered the book on Hoak—pitch him high inside fastballs.

Browning checked the two runners on base, then went into his stretch and let fly his very first major league pitch. Whack! Hoak's bat caught every bit of the high inside fastball and sent it rocketing over the wall at Busch stadium for a home run.

It wasn't just an ordinary four-bagger, either. Browning's first pitch turned into a gopher ball that was hit so hard it busted the red neon eagle in the Budweiser sign on the left field scoreboard.

Browning never recovered from the shock. He walked the next batter, and gave up four more hits and two more runs in two-thirds of an inning before he was yanked.

Cardinals manager Solly Hemus had seen enough, and shipped Browning back to Rochester. The dazed left-hander never pitched in the majors again.

HANGING CURVES

The Most Pitiful Pitching Performances

You can always spot the lousy pitchers. Their curves hang longer than punts while their fastballs move slower than balloons on a still day. Nevertheless, they play an important role in baseball—they fatten batting averages. For "The Most Pitiful Pitching Performances," The Baseball Hall of SHAME inducts the following:

Harley "Doc" Parker

Cincinnati, N.L. • June 21, 1901

Doc Parker sought a second chance as a pitcher so he could leave his mark in baseball. He got his chance. And he left his mark—a black one.

Parker hurled the worst-pitched ball game in major league history.

After three years as a pitcher for the Chicago Cubs, he had a won-loss record that didn't even reach the level of mediocrity. Dropped from the roster after the 1896 season, Parker had disappeared from the major league scene for five long years when he suddenly showed up at the doorstep of the struggling seventh-place Cincinnati Reds.

Parker wanted to pitch again, and they needed help. As it turned out, Parker didn't solve their pitching woes; he compounded them.

Clad in his new Cincinnati uniform, Parker strode to the mound and threw batting practice. Only this wasn't the time for batting practice. It was a major league game against the Brooklyn Dodgers, the previous year's champions. Actually, it didn't matter who faced him. A team of suffragettes could have hit Parker's pitches.

Parker gave up a homer, five doubles, and 20 singles. Everyone who picked up a bat smacked a hit. In fact, the Dodgers were so eager to fatten their batting averages that they ran to the plate. Meanwhile, cold-hearted Reds manager John McPhee left Parker in the game for a battering so bad even the Marquis de Sade would have cried, "Halt!"

Brooklyn scored at will in every inning, ripping 26 hits and tallying 21 runs. By the eighth inning, they grew tired of running the bases, so they just tapped at the ball halfheartedly. According to the *Brooklyn Daily*

Eagle game account, "(The Dodgers) allowed themselves to be retired without attempting to run out the hits, which were fielded slowly and painfully by the tired and weary Cincinnatis (sic)."

When he staggered off the mound at game's end, Parker had established two pitching records that still stand—a National League mark for most runs given up, and a major league record for most hits allowed.

The next day, there was a brief notice buried at the bottom of the *Daily Eagle* sports page: "The Cincinnati Reds announced they released Harley 'Doc' Parker today."

Chuck Stobbs

Washington, A.L. • May 20, 1956

Chuck Stobbs uncorked the wildest pitch in major league history. It was a "tape-measure" throw that sailed 30 feet toward the first base side of home plate—and landed 17 rows up in the stands!

The Washington Senators left-hander was pitching a shutout in the bottom of the fourth inning against the Detroit Tigers. But with one out, he gave up two hits and a walk to load the bases.

Stobbs didn't want to give batter Bob Kennedy anything good to hit. The hurler need not have worried. He wound up and unleashed a pitch that was so wild it crossed two time zones and was tracked by NORAD. It cost him a run as each of the runners gleefully moved up 90 feet.

"I was so surprised," recalled Stobbs, who lost the game 4–2. "I didn't know if I should dig a hole and try to hide under the mound or what the hell to do. All I could do was stand there and wait for the umpire to throw me a new ball."

How did it happen? "As I was winding up, I hit myself on the side of the leg so the ball was right on my fingertips. There was nothing else I could do except go ahead and throw the ball and that's where it ended up.

"Nobody said much to me when I came off the mound. They knew better."

Hugh "Losing Pitcher" Mulcahy

Philadelphia-Pittsburgh, N. L. • 1935–40, 1945–47

There wasn't any one thing that was particularly bad about Hugh Mulcahy's pitching—other than his won-loss record. How else could a guy earn the nickname "Losing Pitcher"?

The Philadelphia sportswriters, never known for their kindness toward the Phillies, saddled him with a moniker that he never lived down. Because he lost two out of every three games (45–89), the Western Union

ticker line score of his games most often ended with "Losing pitcher—
Mulcahy." After awhile, whenever he made an appearance on the mound, a
chant went up in the press box: "Now pitching for Philadelphia, Losing
Pitcher Mulcahy."

Part of his trouble was that he pitched for a pathetic team, the Phillies,
during the years when they needed to climb a ladder to see the bottom of
the league.

Mulcahy was hampered by another problem. He didn't start out as a
pitcher. He was really a shortstop—one whose long legs got mixed up
with ground balls and whose hits were as common as Philadelphia's
pennant-winning years. However, he was big and he had a strong arm.

Mulcahy was given a tryout in front of Phillies manager Jimmy Wilson.
After watching Mulcahy throw, Wilson shook his head, turned to his
assistant, and said, "Doesn't know how to stand on the rubber, doesn't
know how to throw his fastball and has no idea of control."

So, in a move that helps explain the Phillies misfortunes back then,
Wilson signed up Mulcahy as a pitcher. Tossing him into game after game,
Wilson told Mulcahy, "You'll have to learn your lessons losing."

Mulcahy tried to do what he was told—learn by losing.

He never did enjoy a winning season. During a woeful four-year stretch from
1937–40, Mulcahy suffered consecutive losing seasons of 8–18,10–20,
9–16, and 13–22. The 1940 season was a real heartbreaker. On July 31, he
owned a 12–10 record and was convinced he would finally shed his
embarrassing nickname. In fact, he set his sights on winning 20 games. He
pitched with all his heart—and lost 12 straight games, finally breaking the
streak in his final start of the year. He ended up with the most defeats of
any pitcher that season—22.

To make matters worse, he got drafted. Although he could have obtained a deferment, he figured he'd take a year off from baseball and then come back with renewed vigor to improve his record. So he joined the Army on March 8, 1941.

But "Losing Pitcher" was true to his name. Three months before his scheduled discharge, the United States declared war on Japan. Unwittingly, Mulcahy became the first big leaguer to enter World War II—and one of the last to get out.

Tom Gorman   Mark Freeman
George Brunet

Kansas City, A. L. • April 22, 1959

It was the sorriest exhibition of pitching control ever seen in one inning.

Kansas City A's hurlers Tom Gorman, Mark Freeman, and George Brunet were so wild they couldn't find home plate with a compass.

In one deplorable inning, the struggling pitchers walked 10 batters and hit another while allowing the visiting Chicago White Sox to score 11 runs *on only one single.* What's worse, eight of those runs were forced in by bases-loaded walks. (For this reason, the A's performance is even more shameful than that of the Washington Senators record-setting 11 free passes in one inning on September 11, 1949.)

The White Sox were winning 8–6 in the seventh inning when a hit and three errors brought in two runs and put a runner on third base. Gorman could have escaped further damage if the strike zone had been high and outside. But it wasn't, and he started the pitiful base-on-balls procession.

Gorman walked two batters in a row to load the bases, and then threw two straight balls to the next hitter before manager Harry Craft yanked Gorman and brought in Freeman. Whatever pitching disease afflicted Gorman was caught by Freeman. Surrounded by White Sox, Freeman tossed two more balls, which finished the walk and forced in the third run. Then he issued two free passes sandwiched around a force-out at home for another two tallies.

Brunet came in to relieve. In keeping with the tradition already established by his colleagues, Brunet forced in the final six runs with a walk, walk, hit batsman (to break up the monotony), walk, strikeout (no big deal, it was the opposing pitcher), walk, walk, and, mercifully, an inning-ending groundout.

Seventeen White Sox came to the plate in the walkathon half inning that took 45 minutes to complete. The A's were out in the field so long they could have homesteaded the place.

The final score: White Sox 20, A's 6.

Paul LaPalme

Chicago, A.L. • May 18, 1957

Paul LaPalme had the easiest pitching assignment ever given a hurler. Just hold the ball. That's all, just hold the ball.

But, incredibly, he didn't. And he blew the game.

With the Chicago White Sox winning 4–3 over the Baltimore Orioles, LaPalme went out to the mound to pitch in the bottom of the ninth inning. His manager, Al Lopez, gave him strict and simple instructions: Stall.

Under a prearranged agreement, the umpires were to halt the game at exactly 10:20 P.M. to give the Sox time to catch a train for Boston. It was 10:18 P.M. when Oriole Dick Williams led off the ninth inning. Unable to think of any creative way to stall, LaPalme threw a strike and a ball.

By now, time was almost up. Just a few seconds remained before the White Sox could leave town a winner. All LaPalme had to do was simply stand there. Or tie his shoelaces. Or pick his nose. Or scratch his butt. He could do anything except throw the ball.

But he threw the ball anyway—and not way outside, or into the ground or any other spot that would have made a hit impossible. No, Paul LaPalme threw the ball right down the pipe, and Dick Williams whacked it with all his might. As the minute hand stroked exactly 10:20 P.M., the ball landed high in the left field bleachers for a dramatic game-tying homer. The umps then called the game with the score knotted at 4–4.

Lopez blew his top like an overheated teakettle. He ranted and raved and stormed into the clubhouse as the White Sox scattered. They had never seen their leader so furious.

Under American League rules, the tie meant the game had to be re-played in its entirety at a later date. The Orioles won the rematch.

As for LaPalme, his time ran out. After that year, he never played in the majors again.

THE WRECKING CREW

Executives Who Wheeled and Dealed
Their Team to Rack and Ruin

*Every year, the front office drafts a blueprint for building a winning
team. But sometimes the plans are drawn up and then carried out with
a wrecking ball. Rather than being raised to lofty heights, the team is
razed to lowly rubble. For "Executives Who Wheeled and Dealed Their
Team to Rack and Ruin," The Baseball Hall of SHAME inducts the
following:*

Harry Frazee

President and Owner • Boston, A. L. • 1917–23

Harry Frazee took control of the Red Sox during their golden age and
blindly led them straight into the dark age.

From 1912 to 1918, Boston was nearly unstoppable, winning four World
Series and finishing second twice. But Frazee, who had a penchant for
backing Broadway flops, was always short of cash. So he turned to his
players for help—by selling or trading them. Fans were understandably
outraged, especially when Frazee shipped the players to Boston's archen-
emy, the formerly mediocre New York Yankees.

In January 1920, Frazee triggered the decline and fall of the Red Sox
when he sold Babe Ruth to the Yanks for $125,000 as well as a guaranteed
$350,000 mortgage on Fenway Park. He also promised to sell the Yankees
more players if needed.

The loss of Ruth so upset the Fenway faithful that they vowed to run
Frazee out of town. By the time they succeeded, it was too late.

In addition to Ruth, Frazee bestowed upon the Yankees such frontline
players as Carl Mays, Waite Hoyt, Wally Schang, and Mike McNally. As
starters in 1921, they helped the Yankees win their very first pennant.
Boston finished fifth.

With each new Frazee deal, the Yankees grew stronger and the Red Sox
grew weaker. The question of the day for angry Boston fans was, "Who did
Frazee get rid of today?" The answer only made them madder.

In return for some cash and a few has-beens, crazy Frazee dealt away to New York the rest of his quality players in 1922 and 1923, including Bullet Joe Bush, Sad Sam Jones, Everett Scott, Jumping Joe Dugan, Elmer Smith, and Herb Pennock.

Frazee left the Red Sox in shambles, mired in the bottom of the league for the next ten years. As for the Boston players he shipped to New York, they built the foundation of the Yankee dynasty.

Dick Wagner

President • Cincinnati, N. L. • 1978–83

Dick Wagner single-handedly dismantled the Big Red Machine and turned it into a battered pushcart.

From 1970 to 1978, the Reds won five division titles, four pennants, and two world championships. In 1975 and 1976, Cincinnati became one of only three teams in the National League to win back-to-back World Series in this century. Yet when the Reds could do no better than second in 1977 and 1978, Wagner shocked the baseball world by firing manager Sparky Anderson, the leader who built and ran the Big Red Machine.

Wagner further stunned fans by refusing to pay the fair market value of superstar Pete Rose, the most beloved player in Reds history. So Rose signed with the Phillies as a free agent. To prove he was a fair person, Wagner wouldn't give other Reds stars the money they deserved, either. As a result, starters George Foster, Ken Griffey, Tony Perez, and Joe Morgan played out their options or were traded for less than their full value.

It was no surprise that the Reds suffered one of the greatest collapses in the annals of baseball in 1982. After a winning percentage of .611 in 1981, the team finished last the next year, with an abysmal .377 percentage. Their 61–101 record was the worst in the history of the major league's oldest franchise. Adding to their woes, attendance dropped to barely half of what it had been five years earlier.

Wagner's tenure as president was best summed up by an editorial cartoon in the *Cincinnati Enquirer.* It depicts Mickey Mouse chatting with Wagner while an observer says, "I've always wondered where Wagner gets his ideas."

Arnold Johnson

President and Owner • Kansas City, A. L. • 1955–60

Arnold Johnson was the owner of the A's, but he acted more like an employee of the Yankees. Johnson played the stooge for the Yankees, allowing them to scandalously manipulate and plunder Kansas City as though it was their farm club.

Under Johnson's five-year reign, the A's made 16 trades and transactions with the Yankees, involving a total of 56 players. During that period, New York finished first four times; Kansas City's best finish was sixth.

Johnson, a vending machine company executive, didn't know much about baseball. It didn't matter. All he had to do was answer the phone when the Yankees called and follow orders like a dutiful servant.

Occasionally, Johnson allowed the Yankees to ship a young player to the A's so the player could develop his skills away from pennant race pressure. Once he matured, he was traded back. Such an arrangement worked for New York pitcher Ralph Terry, who went to Kansas City in 1957 for two years of seasoning before the Yankees reacquired him in 1959. Terry sparkled as a starter on New York's pennant-winning teams of 1960–64.

When the Yankees needed a new player, they first went shopping in Kansas City. If they found their man, Johnson would deal him to New York no matter how valuable the player was to the A's. For example, in August 1958, the A's were enjoying their finest season ever in Kansas City (2½

AP/Wide World Photo

games out of fourth place) when the Yankees called Johnson and said they wanted pitcher Murry Dickson. Even though Dickson was the second best pitcher on the team, with a 9–5 record, Johnson traded him to the Yanks for an obscure minor leaguer. The A's finished in seventh place.

Once the Yankees had no more use for Kansas City-traded players such as Dickson, Art Ditmar, and Harry Simpson, they were simply dealt back to Johnson's A's.

Among Yankee stars who came through the Johnson pipeline were Roger Maris, Hector Lopez, Clete Boyer, Ryne Duren, and Bobby Shantz.

Johnson had been wheeling and dealing with Yankee owners Del Webb and Dan Topping even before he bought the A's. Webb and Topping held a second mortgage of Johnson's totaling $2.9 million. Johnson headed the corporation that owned Yankee Stadium. And it was Webb's construction company that remodeled Kansas City's stadium to meet major league specifications.

Was it any wonder that Johnson was a Yankee puppet?

Spec Richardson

General Manager • Houston, N.L. • 1968–75

The more Spec Richardson tried to build up his team, the more he tore it down.

During his tenure, the Astros finished in the first division only once. That's because nearly every major deal Richardson made backfired. He traded away enough talent to fill an All-Star lineup in return for stumble-bums who didn't even belong on the farm team.

Richardson stood alone when it came to giving up exceptional talent and getting little or nothing in return. He traded away such outstanding players as John Mayberry, Jim Wynn, Mike Marshall, Mike Cuellar, Rusty Staub, Jerry Reuss, and Dave Giusti for over-the-hillers and babes-in-the-woods.

Houston fans decried his trades. But Cincinnati fans adored them. As the Astros general manager, Richardson unwittingly provided the missing parts for the Big Red Machine. Before the 1972 season, he swapped Joe Morgan, Denis Menke, Cesar Geronimo, and Jack Billingham for Lee May, Tommy Helms, and Jimmy Stewart. The four ex-Astros all made the Reds starting lineup, and the team vaulted from fourth to first while Houston, minus the talent-laden quartet, finished a distant second. The following year, the Reds repeated as Western Division champs. Houston tumbled to fourth and didn't recover until Richardson left.

When he was fired in 1975, Houston fans breathed a sigh of relief that he didn't have time to crate the Astrodome and send it to Cleveland in exchange for antiquated Municipal Stadium.

THE FALL FOLLIES

The Most Atrocious World Series Performances

The World Series isn't always all that it's cracked up to be. Naturally, the lords of baseball want everyone to believe that the October extravaganza showcases the leagues' two best teams, with dazzling fielding, thrilling baserunning, dynamite hitting, and awesome pitching. In truth, the Fall Classic is often the Classic Fall from grace to disgrace for so-called champions. For "The Most Atrocious World Series Performances," The Baseball Hall of SHAME inducts the following:

Detroit Tigers vs. Pittsburgh Pirates

1909

No World Series was ever more shameful—in blood, bickering, and bumbling. Convict riots have been fought with less mayhem than this Series, which left a body count of at least a dozen hurt—eight seriously enough to require medical attention.

Batters spent as much time in the dirt ducking beanballs as they did swinging at pitches. Vengeful pitchers, more intent on getting even than getting outs, managed to drill ten batters in the head and ribs.

The base paths turned into a no-man's-land where fielders caught more flying spikes than grounders. No one stole a base or tagged a runner without paying a price in flesh and blood. That was never made clearer than in the fourth game, when Detroit's Ty Cobb tried to swipe second base. As he took his lead off first, Cobb yelled to shortstop Honus Wagner, "Hey, Kraut-head! I'm coming down on the next pitch!" Sure enough, Cobb, who never left home without sharpened spikes, took off, and slid viciously into second with his spikes so high they slashed Wagner across the bridge of his nose. But Wagner stood his ground and retaliated by smashing the ball smack into Cobb's face, splitting his lip and loosening his teeth.

The top of the ninth inning of the sixth game looked like a gang war. Trailing 5–3 with no one out, the Pirates put runners on first and third. Chief Wilson bunted, and when Tigers first baseman Tommy Jones reached for the fielder's throw, Wilson slammed into Jones and flattened him. The first baseman was carried off the field unconscious.

The score was now 5–4. The Pirates had runners on the corners and no one out. On the next play, Bill Abstein tried to score from third on a ground ball. However, catcher Charley Schmidt blocked the plate and tagged him out, but not before Abstein's spikes slashed open the catcher's leg.

Moments later, Chief Wilson tried to steal third on a strikeout. Though he was nailed for the final out of the game, he managed to demonstrate his spike-wielding skill by carving up the leg of third baseman George Moriarty. Moriarty saw red. Like Ninja warriors in baseball uniforms, Moriarty and Wilson kicked and slashed at each other, even though the game was over.

The carnage raged into the decisive seventh and final game. The Pirates' Bobby Byrne led off by getting plunked with a Wild Bill Donovan fastball, and was sacrificed to second. Then Byrne tried to take out Moriarty in an attempted steal of third. Byrne crashed into the third baseman like a runaway locomotive. Moriarty was badly shaken, but not as badly as Byrne, who was carried off the field with an injured ankle.

The game degenerated into a "let's get Moriarty" campaign. In the second inning, on a play at third, Abstein ripped open Moriarty's knee with his spikes. Eventually, the wounded Moriarty had to leave the game. It took 12 stitches to close the gash.

Besides bloodshed, the Series was marred by constant bickering. The umpire-baiting was so fierce that the National Commission, baseball's ruling body at the time, fined Pirates manager Fred Clarke and five other players for their vociferous arguing. Their lack of respect for umpires was typified by a squabble in the fourth game. Pittsburgh second baseman John Miller touched off a fracas when he was called out on strikes and had to be restrained by his teammates from taking a poke at umpire Bill Klem.

As if that wasn't enough to blacken the eye of the Series, the Pirates and Tigers worked hard at beating themselves. The blundering players muffed easy grounders, dropped routine pop flies, and threw wildly to rack up a modern-day Series record of 34 errors, 19 by the Tigers and 15 by the Pirates.

Adding further shame to the fall classic were the two players who received the most attention—Detroit's Ty Cobb and Pittsburgh's Bill Abstein.

Cobb had refused to accompany his team on the train from Detroit to Pittsburgh for the fifth game because the train traveled via Cleveland. He wanted to avoid Cleveland at all costs because he had heard that authorities planned to arrest him when the train stopped there. He learned that the grand jury had issued an indictment against him for felonious assault over a fight he had with a hotel watchman earlier in the season. Cobb traveled to Pittsburgh by way of Buffalo.

Abstein had troubles of his own. He almost blew the Series for the

Pirates. The first baseman was guilty of five errors, all muffed throws. Furthermore, he batted only .233, and fanned 10 times, usually in the clutch. At least Pirate boss Barney Dreyfuss showed some compassion for Abstein. Dreyfuss waited until after the team's world championship celebration to fire him.

Roger Peckinpaugh

Shortstop • Washington, A. L. • 1925

On the eve of the 1925 World Series, Roger Peckinpaugh was named the American League's Most Valuable Player. It was quite a feather in his cap. But he couldn't wear the cap for long; the goat horns he sprouted in the Series grew much too large.

Peckinpaugh set a futility record that no butter-fingered Hall of Shamer has come close to matching—he pecked and pawed his way to eight errors in one World Series.

Playing as if his glove was made of Portland cement, the worst fielder in the history of the Fall Classic fumbled away three games. As a result, the Pittsburgh Pirates overcame a three-games-to-one deficit to win the world championship right out from under the stunned Washington Senators.

Peck's Bad Boy ranged to his right and to his left and deep in the hole to bungle balls throughout the Series.

He blew the second game in the eighth inning. With the score knotted at 1–1, Peckinpaugh bobbled Eddie Moore's easy grounder. Moments later, Kiki Cuyler belted a homer, scoring Moore ahead of him as the Pirates won 3–2.

In the sixth game, Peckinpaugh's botchery wiped out a 2–0 Washington lead. After Eddie Moore walked in the third inning, Max Carey hit a double-play ball to Peckinpaugh, but the shortstop booted it, leaving both runners safe. A sacrifice, an infield out (which would have been the third out of the inning), and a single drove home two unearned runs. Pittsburgh won 3–2 to even the Series.

It seemed impossible that Peckinpaugh could play any worse, but he did. In the deciding game, Washington held a 6–4 lead in the seventh inning when, once again, Peckinpaugh was afflicted with the dropsies. Moore hit a high pop-up to Peckinpaugh, who was ready to make a routine catch—routine, that is, for most fielders. He muffed it. His error was followed by a double and a triple that tied the score at 6–6.

In the top of the eighth, however, Peckinpaugh smashed a homer to give the Senators a 7–6 lead. Would Peck redeem himself for his disastrous miscues? Nope.

With two out in the bottom of the eighth, Pittsburgh tied the game with back-to-back doubles. Then Moore walked and Carey rapped an easy grounder to Peckinpaugh. The snakebitten shortstop scooped it up, but as he ran to touch second for the simple force-out on Moore, Peckinpaugh stumbled and dropped the ball. His eighth error filled the bases and set the stage for Cuyler, who promptly doubled home the two winning runs. The Pirates won the Series with a 9–7 victory, compliments of Peckinpaugh's four unearned runs.

Needless to say, there was no dinner in Washington to celebrate Peckinpaugh's MVP award.

Curt Flood

Outfielder • St. Louis, N. L. • Oct. 10, 1968

Curt Flood belongs to the Meat Cutter's Union for the way he butchered the St. Louis Cardinals' bid for the 1968 world championship.

In a scoreless duel in the seventh game against the Detroit Tigers, Flood twice carved his name in the annals of World Series ignobility.

The first screw-up came in the sixth inning, after Flood beat out an infield hit. Flood, representing the potential winning run, was picked off first like a sharpshooter's tin can. He should have been more alert because teammate Lou Brock had been picked off earlier in the inning. Flood's lame post-game excuse? "I just didn't think he'd throw over to first."

But the botchery for which Flood will long be remembered occurred in the seventh inning of the scoreless tie, when he misjudged a fly ball to center. With two on and two out for Detroit, Jim Northrup hit a line drive that was well within Flood's reach. Flood took three quick steps in, then braked quickly and changed directions. He retreated toward the wall, but it was too late. The ball sailed over his head for a cheap triple, and the two winning runs crossed the plate. Moments later, Northrup scored. That's all the Tigers needed. They whipped the Cardinals 4–1 for the world championship.

No truer words were spoken when Flood said, "What it all amounts to is I fouled up."

Boston Fans

Oct. 3, 1903

No World Series fans were ever more belligerent or created more havoc than the uncontrollable rabble-rousers who mobbed Boston's Huntington Avenue Baseball Grounds.

Before the start of the third game of the Series between the Boston Red Sox and the Pittsburgh Pirates, thousands of non-paying fans crashed the park by hopping over the fence. Once inside, they milled about in the outfield.

Police were called in, but their attempt to clear the field of the trouble-makers was futile. The crowd teased horse-mounted patrolmen and actually threatened some of the outnumbered cops. Ten minutes before game time, the gate-crashers rushed into a grandstand already full with 18,000 paying spectators.

"This resulted in sundry punches and several severe tumbles," said *The Boston Globe* on the following day. "The police thought it time to be a bit more drastic, and the fresh young men who led the rush had their clothes tousled a bit and were made to see stars which no astronomer has yet mapped.

"In checking this assault, the seat holders in the first rows of the grandstand took part. They pushed at first, but when their pushes were replied to with blows, they let out with right- and left-handed bunches of fives.

"The police in the rear swatted several climbers on bent places which they exposed in climbing and the way the victims grabbed themselves when hit suggested the touch of a white hot brand ... The police, having no fears of fracturing a skull, hit hard."

Police reinforcements arrived and used the players' baseball bats to bang fans over their toes and across their shins. Meanwhile, fence-hopping intruders continued to stream into the park.

The outfield was never cleared. Nevertheless, the game was played, but with an added last-minute rule stating that balls hit into the crowd were two-base hits. As a result, routine fly balls to the mob-lined outfield fell for doubles. Taking advantage of the cheap hits, the Pirates beat the Red Sox, 4–2.

Although the fans in Boston created havoc, their counterparts in Pittsburgh were far from perfect. In the sixth game of the Series, the fans tried to fluster the visiting Red Sox by flinging baskets full of shredded paper into the breeze. The scraps filled the air and covered the field, but they didn't bother Boston pitcher Bill Dinneen. He won 6–3. *The Boston Globe* couldn't help but take a potshot at the Pirate faithful: "The Boston rooters are educated in the finer points of their art, and never . . . bothered an opposing pitcher."

No, they just bothered the whole Series.

Aaron Ward

Second baseman • New York, A. L. • Oct. 13, 1921

Aaron Ward ran for glory, but made a wrong turn.

In the bottom of the ninth inning of the final game of the World Series, the New York Giants were leading the Yankees by the slimmest of margins, 1–0. With one out, Ward walked, representing the tying run for the Yanks. Ward wanted to make something happen. He did. He made something bad happen.

Teammate Frank Baker slashed a hard grounder that second baseman Johnny Rawlings snared on his knees and recovered in time to nail Baker at first by an eyelash. Meanwhile, with the recklessness of a kamikaze pilot, Ward roared around second base and headed for third. Even a rookie would know enough not to risk the third out by foolishly trying to advance two bases on an infield out. But Ward was no rookie. He was no speed merchant either, having stolen all of six bases the whole year.

First baseman George Kelly rifled a throw to third baseman Frankie Frisch, who slapped the easy tag on Ward. Third out. End of game. End of Series. End of a stupid play.

Max Flack   Phil Douglas
Outfielder   Pitcher
Chicago, N. L. • Sept. 9, 1918

Flack & Douglas. Sounds like a wrecking company. It *was* a wrecking company. The two Chicago Cubs demolished their own team's chances of winning the crucial fourth game of the World Series.

Chicago had already lost two of the games to the Boston Red Sox. A win would even the Series; a loss would put the Cubs in a deep hole. By the time Flack & Douglas were through, the Cubs were all but buried.

Flack started the destruction in the first inning. After singling, he was picked off, caught napping by catcher Sam Agnew. In the third inning, Flack was as alert as a finalist in a dance marathon and again was picked off, this time at second base, by pitcher Babe Ruth.

Flack continued to lead the Cubs to ruin in the fourth inning, when, with two out, Boston put runners on second and third, bringing the ever-dangerous Babe Ruth to bat. Chicago pitcher George Tyler signaled to Flack in right field to move back toward the fence. Flack shifted only a few inches. Again, Tyler waved to Flack to play deeper, but the outfielder stubbornly refused.

Even though Ruth spent part of the year as a starting pitcher, he still led the league in homers. None of that mattered to Flack. It should have mattered. Ruth clobbered Tyler's next pitch and the ball sailed over the shallow-playing Flack. By the time Flack tracked down the ball, Ruth had reached third with a standup triple—and the Red Sox had a 2–0 lead. Had Flack listened to his pitcher and played deep, he would have caught Ruth's drive for the third out and Boston wouldn't have scored.

The next time Ruth came to bat, in the seventh inning, Flack played deep enough to need a bleacher ticket. The crowd in Boston laughed derisively when he had to dash in to catch Ruth's sacrifice fly.

In the eighth inning, the Cubs tied the score 2–2 (through no help of Flack, who grounded out as runners held at second and third).

What damage Flack had done to his team, relief pitcher Phil Douglas finished off. When Shufflin' Phil entered the tie game in the bottom of the eighth, he immediately gave up a single to Wally Schang, who then scampered to second on a passed ball.

With the winning run in scoring position, Douglas went to his special pitch—the spitter. He threw it to Harry Hooper, who laid down a nifty bunt. When Douglas fielded the ball, it was so wet and slippery from spit that he lost his grip and threw wildly past first base. Schang raced home easily with the winning tally.

Wrote *The New York Times*, "The trickery pitching of Douglas had turned on him like a boomerang and he succumbed to his own faulty artfulness."

And, thus, the company of Flack & Douglas helped complete the fourth game demolition of the Chicago Cubs.

BACKSTOP BLOCKHEADS

The Most Bungled Plays by Catchers

The catcher's mask, chest protector, and shin guards are called the "tools of ignorance" for a good reason. Anybody with an ounce of brains knows better than to crouch for 2½ hours behind the plate getting whacked by foul tips, trying to stop 100 mph fastballs, and being bowled over by base runners. For "The Most Bungled Plays by Catchers," The Baseball Hall of SHAME inducts the following:

Choo Choo Coleman

Philadelphia-New York, N. L. • 1961–66

No player enhanced the blockhead image of catchers more than Choo Choo Coleman.

Choo Choo seemed to whistle-stop along the train tracks of life without a caboose. One of the original Mets, he had a little boy's smile, a strange talent for hitting foul "home runs," a madcap scrambling style behind the plate, and an unnerving knack for making teammates lose confidence in him. Especially when it came to signals.

In flashing their finger signs to the pitcher, catchers often go through a complicated series of numbers. Coleman never appeared to get the hang of it. Met coaches became so exasperated they planned to paint his fingers—blue for fastball, red for curve, green for change-up—so he wouldn't forget.

Umpire Al Barlick couldn't help but laugh during a game in 1962 when he saw Choo Choo go through a series of signs; when the Met pitcher nodded that he had the sign, Coleman looked down at his own fingers to see what it was.

Choo Choo was also a dud at the plate. In 1963, he batted only .178, and manager Casey Stengel knew he couldn't depend on him too much— as a hitter or a conversationalist.

Coleman's vocabulary consisted largely of "yup," "nope," and "hi." He called everyone "Bub" because he wasn't very good at remembering names.

Met infielder Charlie Neal proved Coleman's memory lapses to a group of sportswriters during the first day of spring training in 1963. "Watch this," said Neal, who had roomed with Coleman on the road the year before. "I'll go up to Choo Choo and he won't know my name." Neal sauntered over to Coleman, exchanged hellos, and said, "Choo Choo, I bet you don't know who I am."

"Yup, Bub," said Coleman. "You're number four."

In his first spring training camp, Choo Choo had everyone shaking their heads. In an interview during a pre-game telecast, Ralph Kiner asked Coleman, "What's your wife's name—and what's she like?"

Replied Choo Choo, "Her name is Mrs. Coleman—and she likes me."

Aaron Robinson

Detroit, A. L. • Sept. 24, 1950

In the final week of the season, the Tigers still had a chance to knock the mighty Yankees off their first place perch. But when Aaron Robinson fell asleep at the switch, Detroit's pennant dream was derailed.

The Tigers were only two games behind New York when they came into Cleveland's Municipal Stadium to play the Indians. The game turned into a classic pitchers' duel and went into the bottom of the tenth inning tied 1–1.

Indians pitcher Bob Lemon led off the inning with a booming triple. Tiger manager Red Rolfe had no choice but to order pitcher Ted Gray to walk the next two batters intentionally and load the bases for a possible force at home.

Cleveland's Larry Doby then hit a pop-up for the first out. The next batter, Luke Easter, hit a grounder to first baseman Don Kolloway. He fielded the ball, stepped on the bag for the second out, and then threw home, hoping to complete a game-saving double play.

Lemon, coming from third, was a good five feet from home when Robinson took the throw and triumphantly stepped on the plate. Incredibly, Robinson made no attempt to tag the runner as he should have because Kolloway, by stepping on first base before throwing home, had taken off the force.

Robinson just stood like a rock as Lemon slid across the plate at the catcher's feet for the winning run.

The devastating loss helped eliminate the Tigers from the pennant race. It came as no surprise when Robinson was traded the following year.

Hank Gowdy

New York, N. L. • Oct. 10, 1924

With the gracefulness Hank Gowdy showed in the seventh and final game of the 1924 Series, the Giants catcher would probably have tripped over his own shadow.

His clumsiness cost his team the world championship.

Gowdy was behind the plate in the bottom of the twelfth inning of a 3–3 tie. Up to bat for the Washington Senators stepped weak-hitting Muddy Ruel, who had managed to get only two hits in 21 trips to the plate during the Series.

Muddy lifted a high, lazy foul back of the plate for what appeared to be an easy out. Like a good catcher, Gowdy threw his mask off and went after the pop-up. But, like a bad catcher, he threw his mask right in his path.

As he circled under the foul, Gowdy pulled a boner seldom seen in baseball—he stepped on his mask and got his foot stuck. Keeping his eye on the ball, he desperately tried to shake off the discarded hardware. By now the ball was descending and Gowdy was panicking. As if he was doing a poor imitation of Long John Silver, Gowdy hobbled on his mask and stumbled as the ball dropped harmlessly beside him.

Inspired by the second chance at the plate that Gowdy had given him, Ruel rapped a sharp double. Earl McNeely then hit a bad-hop single and Ruel raced home with the winning run—and the world championship.

Bob Tillman

Boston, A. L. • May 12, 1967

Bob Tillman spent hours practicing throws to second base so he could shoot down thieving runners. He didn't mow down all that many base stealers, but he did manage once to plug his own pitcher.

Boston Red Sox relief pitcher John Wyatt came in to pitch in the eighth inning of a tight ball game against the visiting Detroit Tigers. Fans gave him an ovation because he had yet to be scored on in eight appearances that year.

Wyatt walked Al Kaline, who then broke for second base two pitches later. Tillman cut loose with a strong throw as Wyatt ducked and turned toward second to see how good his catcher's marksmanship was. The pitcher painfully learned it was off target.

The throw struck Wyatt smack in the back of his head! The ball bounced all the way to the on-deck circle on the first base side of the field. As the amazed fans watched in fascinated horror, Wyatt staggered around on the mound. By the time Tillman retrieved the ball, Kaline had reached third base.

Tillman received an error and Wyatt received a headache. But the plucky pitcher stayed in the game. The next batter, Willie Horton, hit a sacrifice fly for the first run of the year off Wyatt. The run was not only unearned but also crucial; the Red Sox lost 5–4.

Not in recent memory had anyone ever seen a catcher throw a beanball at a pitcher.

Paul Ratliff

Minnesota, A. L. • April 25, 1970

The very first rule a catcher learns is that on a dropped third strike he must tag the batter or throw to first. Twins catcher Paul Ratliff must have been playing hooky when that lesson was given. His blunder allowed a Detroit batter to reach third on a strikeout.

During a game against the Tigers, Ratliff, a rookie at the time, trapped the ball in the dirt after Detroit's Earl Wilson swung and missed for a third strike. Ratliff did not tag Wilson. Since he thought it was the third out, Ratliff rolled the ball back toward the mound and ran into the dugout while the rest of the team started running off the field.

George Resinger, coaching at third for the Tigers, spotted the boo-boo. He waited until most of the Twins were in the dugout and then yelled at Wilson to run. Hardly the fastest human afoot, Wilson made it to first unchallenged. Since the Twins weren't watching, he lumbered to second and then headed for third. By this time, Twins left fielder Brant Alyea, who was slowly trotting in from his position, suddenly realized that Wilson was trying to score. Alyea ran to the mound, picked up the ball and shouted for help. Wilson was around third when Alyea threw to shortstop Leo Cardenas, who had raced out of the dugout to cover home. Then Alyea ran to cover third.

Unfortunately for Detroit, Wilson suddenly pulled a hamstring muscle and was tagged out by Alyea on Cardenas's return throw.

On his way back to catcher's school, Ratliff said, "I didn't know you had to tag the runner in that case."

Johnny Peacock

Boston, A. L. • Sept. 12, 1942

Johnny Peacock was conked on the head because he didn't use his brain.

The embarrassing—and painful—moment occurred in the bottom of the eighth inning as his Boston Red Sox held a slim 4–3 lead over the Cleveland Indians. When the Tribe put runners on first and second, Peacock decided to switch signals with his pitcher Joe Dobson so the runner on second would have difficulty stealing the signs.

But Peacock forgot one important thing. He failed to inform Dobson of the switched signals.

Behind the plate, Peacock flashed one finger, which to him now meant "curveball." But to the unknowing Dobson, it was the fastball signal they had been using the whole game.

While Peacock moved his glove low in expectation of a curveball, Dobson fired a blazing fastball right in the strike zone. Unable to get his mitt up in time, Peacock was nailed right in the head. The ball bounced off his forehead and bounded to the screen behind home plate. Peacock staggered after the ball while players in both dugouts reeled with laughter.

It wasn't funny to Peacock. He suffered a throbbing headache. That was quite understandable, considering Dobson's remark to reporters after the game, "That pitch was my very best fast one."

Dave Engle

Minnesota, A. L. • May 15, 1984

Minnesota Twins catcher Dave Engle caught what he thought was a nifty shutout. But he left his position a wee bit too soon—and caught hell.

With one out in the top of the ninth inning and the Twins ahead 1–0, the Toronto Blue Jays had runners on first and second when pinchhitter Rick Leach hit what appeared to be a game-ending double-play grounder. But first baseman Kent Hrbek dropped the relay throw. Meanwhile, Blue Jay runner Mitch Webster steamed from second base around third and headed for home. Hrbek then threw to the plate—but no one was there.

Where was Engle? He was out at the mound congratulating relief pitcher Ron Davis! Prematurely.

Because the catcher deserted his post, Hrbek's throw sailed to the backstop, and the tying run scored. Toronto went on to win 5–2 in ten innings.

A rather ashamed Engle said after the game, "I went out to congratulate Ron Davis. I took my eye off the umpire. Then I heard everybody screaming and I couldn't figure out what it was all about. I turned around and saw the ball was going back toward home plate."

Engle was in no mood to hear Toronto catcher Buck Martinez's assessment of the chuckle-headed play: "You just can't take anything for granted in this game. Sooner or later it will catch up with you and you'll get embarrassed."

BASEBALL'S MBAS

Dishonorary Degrees for Managers of Blundering Actions

Those who can, do. Those who can't, teach. Those who can't do either, manage. And sometimes they don't do that very well. In fact, they'd have trouble managing a Little League team. The lucky ones can mishandle the players, screw up the lineup, make the wrong moves, and still win because the team has talent. But if they have no gifted players to hide behind, their mismanagement becomes glaring enough for all to see. For "Dishonorary Degrees for Managers of Blundering Actions," The Baseball Hall of SHAME inducts the following:

John McGraw

New York, N. L. • Aug. 7, 1906

Giants manager John McGraw was born to hate umpires. He insulted them, he threatened them, he fought them. But when he decided to show one umpire who was boss, McGraw was shot down—needlessly causing his team a loss by forfeit.

The trouble started on August 6, 1906, in a home game against the Chicago Cubs at the Polo Grounds. Umpire Jimmy Johnstone ejected the hot-tempered manager after he argued violently over a close call at the plate in a game that the Giants lost 3–1.

McGraw decided to flex his muscle and keep Johnstone from umpiring the next day. Remembering that several irate fans threw bottles at Johnstone in protest over the call, McGraw concocted a scheme. He asked Police Inspector Sweeney to issue a statement saying that the police thought it would be unsafe for Johnstone to appear at the game. Sweeney refused. But that didn't stop McGraw.

The next day the gatekeeper, on McGraw's orders, barred Johnstone from entering, using the excuse that the umpire's safety was in jeopardy. Without Johnstone, the other arbiter, Bob Emslie, refused to umpire the game. That was fine with McGraw.

Inside the Polo Grounds, McGraw wanted the game run his way, with

each team picking a player to act as umpire. McGraw chose his utility man, Sam Strang. But the Cubs would have none of this foolishness, and the team gathered its equipment and headed for the clubhouse.

McGraw grinned and signaled to Strang, who promptly announced that the game had been forfeited to New York, 9–0. Meanwhile, outside the park, Johnstone announced that he had forfeited the game—to Chicago, 9–0.

Now both teams claimed the forfeit, but McGraw was confident he'd win the showdown. The following day, National League president Harry Pulliam rejected McGraw's bullying tactics and upheld Johnstone's forfeit decision.

When he returned to the Polo Grounds for the next Cubs-Giants game, Johnstone expected the worst. To his surprise, as he walked onto the field, the fans began cheering him in recognition of his courage and principles. While the umpire proudly doffed his cap to acknowledge the applause, McGraw sat in the dugout grim-faced, a loser in a fight that should never have been fought.

Preston Gomez

San Diego, N. L. • July 21, 1970

Clay Kirby was just three outs away from pitching a once-in-a-lifetime no-hitter. But he never got the chance to finish. Ignoring a golden opportunity to give his last-place team and the suffering fans a needed psychological lift, manager Preston Gomez yanked Kirby from the game.

Kirby, a promising 22-year-old hurler, had pitched brilliantly for eight innings against the second-place Mets. Although Kirby had given up no hits, San Diego was losing 1–0 on a first-inning walk, two stolen bases, and an RBI groundout.

In the bottom of the eighth inning with two out and no one on base, it was Kirby's turn at bat. Kirby was on the verge of a public relations bonanza for the struggling second-year expansion team. The Padres were 29 games out of first and desperate to draw customers (in fact, there were times when the only noise in the stands came from Marine recruits who cheered on orders from their drill sergeant). More than anything, the Padres needed something to awaken local interest in the team; a no-hitter would have been just the tonic for the sick franchise.

But Preston Gomez didn't care about such matters. As Kirby started up to the plate with his bat, Gomez called him back. The hometown crowd of 10,373 booed lustily when Clarence Gaston went up to pinch-hit. They booed even louder when he struck out.

A riled, thick-set fan jumped down from the box seats and faced the San Diego dugout, looking for Gomez. But members of the team were not well known, so he didn't recognize the manager. The police quickly hustled the intruder off the field. As he was led away through the stands, fans cheered him, shook his hand, and patted him on the back.

When Padres relief pitcher Jack Baldschun came in to pitch in the ninth, the crowd booed. Then, turning on Gomez, the fans chanted, "Go, go, Mets!" The Mets did. Leadoff batter Bud Harrelson singled to left for the Mets first hit, triggering a two-run, three-hit inning—and a 3–0 New York victory.

Gomez had played by the book—one that in this case should have been thrown away.

Chuck Dressen

Brooklyn, N. L. • 1951

Chuck Dressen deliberately violated one of baseball's truest maxims, "Let sleeping dogs lie." It cost him the 1951 pennant.

On August 9, the Dodgers had just walloped the Giants in three straight at Ebbets Field to move 12½ games in front of second place New York.

The Bums figured they had the pennant all sewn up. After the game, they whooped and hollered while Giants manager Leo Durocher and his players listened glumly from their next door dressing room.

"Eat your heart out, Leo!" shouted Dressen through the wall. Then he and his players started singing, "Roll out the barrels ... we've got the Giants on the run!"

The unmerciful taunts fired the Giants into a fury. "Human beings can only take so much and we had a belly-full," Giants captain Al Dark said. "You just can't treat human beings like they treated us and get away with it."

Two days after the stinging defeat, New York launched a 16-game winning streak, and kept driving hard the rest of the season, winning 37 out of their last 44 games to tie Brooklyn. Then, in an historic play-off series, the Giants paid Dressen back for his ridiculing by whipping the Dodgers.

Brooklyn could have avoided the play-offs had Dressen not incurred the wrath of the fourth-place Boston Braves in the last week of the season. In a 15–5 Dodger rout, Jackie Robinson, at Dressen's urging, rubbed salt in the Braves' wounds by stealing home for a totally unnecessary run.

"They made us mad," snarled Braves manager Tommy Holmes after the game. "And they're going to pay for it!" The Braves won the next day, 4–3, depriving the Dodgers of a victory that would have allowed them to avoid the disastrous play-off with the Giants.

After the game in which Robinson stole home, reporters asked Dressen why he had tried to anger other teams. "I like to get them hopping mad," he said. "They make mistakes. Some people say 'let sleeping dogs lie,' but I say to hell with that."

To hell with your theory, Chuck.

Joe McCarthy

Boston, A.L. • Oct. 4, 1948

In the most important game of the year—a winner-take-all play off for the 1948 American League pennant—Joe McCarthy made the most absurd pitching decision ever.

Mulling over his choice of a starter against the Cleveland Indians, the Red Sox manager ignored his starting pitchers—Jack Kramer (18–5), Joe Dobson (16–10), Mel Parnell (15–8), and Ellis Kinder (10–7). Instead, to the shocked disbelief of his team, McCarthy pinned the Boston fortunes on the tired right arm of Denny Galehouse (8–7), a 36-year-old journeyman in the twilight of a mediocre career.

As everyone except McCarthy expected, the Indians pounded Galehouse for four runs and five hits before he staggered off the mound in the fourth inning. Cleveland rolled on to an easy 8–3 victory and a World Series date with the Boston Braves.

No one on the Red Sox ever dreamed that McCarthy would choose Galehouse. Not even Galehouse figured he'd be picked. "He was dumbfounded," recalled Mel Parnell. "He was shagging flies in the outfield during batting practice when McCarthy sent a clubhouse man for him. When Joe told him, Denny went white as a ghost."

Tired from his pre-game workout (which he wouldn't have gone through had he known he was pitching), Galehouse took a rest in the clubhouse. Then he went out to warm up on the sidelines while stunned Fenway Park fans wondered what he was doing there.

Cleveland manager Lou Boudreau later admitted he thought McCarthy was trying to pull a fast one by having the real starting pitcher warm up beneath the stands. Boudreau refused to believe McCarthy had picked Galehouse.

Echoing the sentiments of his Boston teammates, Parnell said, "With everything riding on the game, it didn't make a lot of sense." It sure didn't.

Leo Durocher

Chicago, N. L. • 1969

In the heat of battle, Leo Durocher, field general of the Cubs, went AWOL once too often. It was because of his lack of leadership that his team lost the fight for the 1969 pennant.

The Cubs were leading the pack and eyeballing their first pennant in 24 years when Leo pulled off his first disappearing act on June 18. Shortly after dawn, he sneaked out of the Cubs' hotel in Pittsburgh and returned to Chicago for a high society bachelor bash on the eve of his marriage to Lynn Walker Goldblatt.

The Cubs management didn't know the whereabouts of the absent skipper, so coach Pete Reiser took over. The Cubs lost 3–2. The next day, owner Phil Wrigley learned the truth about Leo's unexcused absence, but forgave him.

Five weeks later, however, on July 26, Durocher skipped out on his team once again. During the early innings of a Cubs-Dodgers game, Leo suddenly became "ill" and left the ball park. He was "sick" the next day, too. The Cubs soon discovered that the supposedly ailing Durocher had spent the weekend visiting his wife's son, Joel, at Camp Ojibwa in Wisconsin. Leo had flown there Saturday afternoon on a chartered plane and returned on Sunday after the Cubs had lost 6–2. Wrigley, demanding an apology, declared, "You can't run a ship without a rudder."

While Leo shrugged off the AWOL incidents and continued to manage, he was also doing commercials and radio shows. Taking a cue from Durocher, the players engaged in an overzealous pursuit of side money. He let them establish a pot for extra money from endorsements and appearance fees, to be split after the season. He even allowed them to hire a business agent, who showed up in the clubhouse almost every day to regale the players with an accounting of how much money was piling up. But the Cubs couldn't see beyond their noses; they would have made more from World Series checks had they concentrated on winning.

Unfortunately, their outside interests and Leo's absences had a crippling effect on the team. The Cubs slipped into a horrible slump and blew their 9½-game, mid-August lead over the Mets. Chicago ended up in second place eight games behind New York.

Had the Cubs not folded in the clutch, Leo's sins might have been forgiven. As it was, his transgressions became a sorry legacy of the Cubs' 1969 season.

BOGUS BABIES

High-Priced Rookies Who Failed Miserably

There was a time when every team just had to have a bonus baby—some peach fuzz-faced teenager who looked spectacular in schoolboy competition. Teams shelled out millions of dollars in bonuses in a frantic scramble to sign these "future stars." More often than not, the teams paid for "shooting stars," judging by the length and direction that their baseball careers took. For "High-Priced Rookies Who Failed Miserably," The Baseball Hall of SHAME inducts the following:

Bruce Swango

Pitcher • Baltimore, A.L. • 1955

In the spring of 1955, major league scouts from eight teams descended on the tiny town of Welch, Oklahoma. Their target: 18-year-old pitcher Bruce Swango, who averaged 17 strikeouts a game in high school and once fanned 23 prep batters in a row.

Declared fellow Oklahoman Mickey Mantle, who had been enlisted as a special recruiter for the Yankees: "He's as fast as Bob Turley."

Mantle was, by far, a better hitter than a recruiter. On May 23, Swango signed with Baltimore for a well-publicized $36,000 bonus and immediately joined the Orioles. Although he suited up for the games, he never threw a pitch in the majors. His fastball was so wild that his Oriole teammates refused to step into the cage against him in batting practice. Furthermore, his curveball didn't curve.

The Orioles were so embarrassed they gave Swango his unconditional release just nine weeks after signing him. They announced to the press that he had suffered an arm injury. Later, the Orioles sheepishly admitted that the story about Swango's injury was nothing but a cover-up. In truth, they soured on him because they had picked a lemon.

Paul Pettit

Pitcher • Pittsburgh, N.L. • 1950

Paul Pettit became baseball's first $100,000 bonus baby when he signed with Pittsburgh. The Pirates paid a stiff price. They got only one career victory out of his expensive left arm.

George Brace Photo

Pettit's story reads like a Hollywood script with a bad ending. In high school, he had good looks, a fastball that hopped, and the classy nickname of the "Wizard of Whiff." He pitched six no-hitters in one high school season and once struck out 27 batters in a 12-inning game.

In 1949, while still in high school, Pettit was approached by Frederick Stephani, a movie producer who wanted to film the life story of an athlete. Convinced that Pettit would eventually make it big, Stephani signed him to a personal services contract for $85,000. Three months later, in 1950, Stephani sold Pettit's contract to the Pirates for $100,000.

A special clause in the contract granted Pettit an additional $750 for a honeymoon trip to Hawaii if Pettit got married, which he did. The contract also called for a movie and TV deal based on his life story once he became a big league star. It was never made.

Unfortunately, Pettit reminded no one of a flash. He did, however, remind everyone of a flash in the pan.

Joe Tepsic

Outfielder • Brooklyn, N.L. • 1946

In 1946, the Dodgers couldn't wait to triumphantly announce the signing of Penn State phenom Joe Tepsic. By the end of the season, they couldn't wait to get rid of him.

In addition to receiving a $17,000 bonus, Tepsic had a contract clause requiring Brooklyn to carry him on its major league roster for the entire year. He played sparingly, going hitless in five at-bats.

In the heat of the pennant race between the Dodgers and Cardinals, Tepsic was too green to be of any help. On behalf of the players, veteran outfielder Dixie Walker asked Tepsic to go to the minors voluntarily so the Dodgers could call up a badly needed pinchhitter. But with total disregard for his team's welfare, Tepsic refused. The Dodgers eventually lost to the Cardinals in a post-season play-off. Understandably, Brooklyn dumped Tepsic. He never played in the majors again.

Billy Joe Davidson

Pitcher • Cleveland, A.L. • 1951

Ever since one of their scouts first spotted Billy Joe Davidson pitching American Legion ball at the precocious age of 12, the Cleveland Indians were determined to sign him.

When he graduated high school in 1951, the Indians obviously considered it a privilege, and even a pleasure, to put up a then whopping $120,000 bonus to secure the young prodigy's services.

What they didn't buy was the next Bob Feller. What they did buy was a human butterball. Billy Joe had been ineligible for sports in his senior year at high school and was totally out of shape when he reported to the Indians. He was 30 pounds overweight and looked as though he had spent his bonus money on all-you-can-eat buffets.

Hampered by his weight problem, Billy Joe never made it out of Class B minor league ball and eventually quit, a failure—albeit a well-to-do failure.

THE MEAN TEAM

The Meanest Players of All Time

Some players are just plain mean. They play as though they left their consciences in the clubhouse. Their actions on and off the field are so heartless that they make Attila the Hun look like a wimp. They walk around with more than chips on their shoulders—they carry 2 × 4s. Maybe they are not so bad once you get to know them ... but why bother? For "The Meanest Players of All Time," The Baseball Hall of SHAME inducts the following:

Art Shires

First Baseman • Chicago-Washington, A.L.; Boston, N.L. • 1928–32

Like the rest of humanity, Art Shires was born with his fist clenched and his mouth open. But unlike most people, he never relaxed the former or shut the latter.

Shires was the bad boy of baseball—a brawler, a drinker, and a nose-thumber of curfews and rules. He called himself "Whataman" and "Art the Great" and insisted everyone else do, too, or they'd find themselves on the receiving end of his fat fists.

Shires had a mean streak that showed itself only on days ending in "y". He punched his way around the American League, beating up opposing players. But throughout the 1929 season, Shires gave his fists a workout mostly on the face of his manager, Lena Blackburne of the Chicago White Sox.

During spring training in March, Blackburne offered to make Shires captain of the team if the rabble-rouser would behave himself. To celebrate, Shires went right out and broke all the training rules. When Blackburne told Shires he could kiss the captaincy good-bye, Shires kissed off Blackburne with a couple of pokes that cost the manager a black eye and the player a suspension.

Then, on May 15, Shires showed up for batting practice wearing a silly red hat. Blackburne ordered him to take it off and grow up. Shires cussed out his manager in front of the team and threatened to run him out of baseball. Blackburne kicked him off the field. Later, when the manager went into the clubhouse, he was ambushed by Shires, who once again beat him up. Shires was fined and suspended for two weeks.

The final fight with his manager came September 13, when the White Sox were in Philadelphia. A drunken Shires was raising a ruckus in his hotel room, using empty bottles as Indian clubs and shouting for more liquor. When Blackburne and Lou Barbour, the team's road secretary, tried to quiet him down, Shires wrangled Blackburne into a headlock while throwing punches at Barbour, who was backed into a corner. Finally, two house detectives piled into the melee. During the struggle, Barbour bit his own thumb, thinking it belonged to Shires. Once again, Blackburne sported a shiner. Shires was soon traded away.

Shires was so tough that one night in 1930 he burst into the police station in Hollywood, California, and challenged officers to throw him out. They threw him in instead. They then charged him with a concealed weapons violation, having found brass knuckles in his pocket.

When Shires ran out of people to fight for spite, he fought for profit. In 1929 he moonlighted as a professional boxer during the off-season. He challenged everybody, even boxing champ Gene Tunney, who had the sense to ignore the loudmouth.

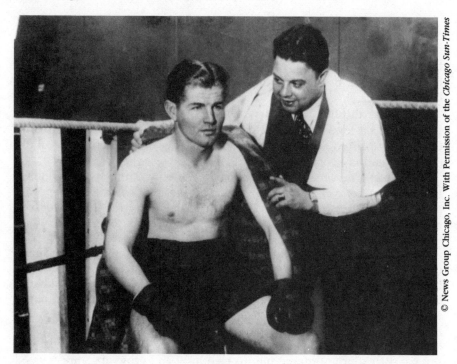

For his bouts, Shires always entered the arena in a crimson robe emblazoned with "ART THE GREAT" in bold white letters on the back.

In his first bout, he took on Mysterious Dave Daly. What was so mysterious about Daly was how he stayed on his feet long enough to make it into the ring. Shires kayoed him in 21 seconds.

When Shires planned to box Chicago Cubs star Hack Wilson for the mythical "major league title," baseball commissioner Kenesaw Mountain Landis stepped forward. He knocked out Shires's brief boxing career with a haymaker edict: "Give up baseball or give up boxing." Shires gave up boxing.

Art the Great's ego was hurt, but not as badly as it was one evening when he attended a Broadway musical. As he strolled down the aisle to his front row theater seat, the audience started to cheer and clap. Shires acknowledged the applause with bows to his left and right. But then, much to his red-faced chagrin, he realized the audience was saluting two true greats who also had just entered the theater—Douglas Fairbanks and Joan Crawford.

Early Wynn

Pitcher • Washington-Cleveland-Chicago, A.L. • 1939–63

Early Wynn was baseball's exorcist—he scared the devil out of batters.

With his thin lips set in a sneer and his dark eyes flashing a sinister glare, the burly 220-pounder earned the title of the meanest man on the mound in his era. He was an ornery cuss with dirt under his nails and blood in his eyes. He threw message pitches that read, "Don't dig in on me, buster, or you'll pay the price."

Wynn regarded every batter as the enemy—even his own teenage son! When Wynn was with Cleveland, he pitched pre-game batting practice to his 15-year-old son Joe. After Joe hit two long shots in a row off his father, the ushers in the empty stands started to clap. The next thing anybody saw was Joe flat on his back in the batting cage, scared stiff by one of Pop's knockdown pitches. "He was leaning in on me," Wynn explained, "and I had to show him who was boss."

Wynn conceded that part of the batter's box belonged to the hitter, "but when he crowds it just that hair, well then, son, he's stepping into my office. And nobody comes in my office without an invitation."

The Yankees' Gil McDougald tried, but only once. During a game, McDougald crowded the plate so much that Wynn complained to the umpire. The man in blue shrugged, noting that the toe of McDougald's shoe still was on the chalk line. "Okay," said Wynn. "If you won't move him, I will." He fired a fastball up and in—and McDougald hit the dirt.

As an intimidator, Wynn was a craftsman, and the brushback was a tool

of his trade. His code required a two-for-one retaliation. Any time one of his teammates was knocked down by an opposing pitcher, Wynn knocked down two opposing batters. "I never throw at a man's head," Wynn once told a reporter. "But," he added, jabbing a big hand in the writer's ribs, "right there, now that's a different story."

Wynn had a rule that when a batter hit one of his pitches back through the box, Wynn countered with a brushback pitch the next time the batter was up. He made absolutely no exceptions.

Once in 1962, for instance, when Wynn was throwing batting practice, White Sox first baseman Joe Cunningham slammed a line drive that missed the hurler by inches. Wynn responded by firing three straight dusters right under Cunningham's chin. Then Wynn let up. After all, Cunningham was a teammate.

During a game against the Yankees, Mickey Mantle whacked a liner between Wynn's legs. Rather than wait until Mantle's next time at bat to get even with a duster, Wynn retaliated immediately. He ordered his first baseman to stand in foul territory behind Mantle. Then, with all his might, Wynn tried to hit Mantle with pickoff throws.

Wynn always got even, on the field and off. One evening in a restaurant, a drunken bore made a pest of himself and spoiled Wynn's dinner. Disgusted, Wynn walked out—but not before dropping a lighted cigarette into the drunk's coat pocket.

For 23 years, Wynn terrorized all who dared cross his path. He gave no quarter. Declared the master of meanness with total sincerity, "I'd knock down my own grandmother if she dug in on me."

John McGraw

Third baseman • Baltimore-St. Louis-New York, N.L.;
Baltimore, A.L. • 1891–1906
Manager • Baltimore, A.L.; Baltimore-New York, N.L. • 1899–1932

John McGraw's ruthlessness was unequaled in baseball. If he couldn't win with good hitting and fielding, he'd win with brutality and malice—by slugging, spiking, gouging, and maiming. His savagery belonged in the Dark Ages. And he played like a raging barbarian.

As a player, McGraw swung his fists as often as his bat. The terrible-tempered, intolerant cutthroat brawled with spectators, umpires, opposing ball players, and even members of his own team.

He deliberately put two players in the hospital during one bloody trip around the bases. The carnage began on a play at second base in an 1894 game against the New York Giants. As the meanest player on the mean Baltimore Orioles, McGraw dug his cleats into second baseman Monte Ward, knocking him into center field and out of the game.

Moments later, McGraw rounded third and headed for home, where catcher Duke Farrell caught the throw and braced for a bone-crunching collision. With the deadly scream of a black belt karate master, McGraw powered his spikes into Farrell's belly. For good measure, McGraw jammed a straight-arm into the catcher's face and tried to gouge his eyes out. Miraculously, Farrell held onto the ball and tagged McGraw out. Then the catcher and Ward were rushed to the hospital.

As a manager, "Little Napoleon" wore meanness like skin. "John J. McGraw on the field was a detriment to baseball until he resigned as Giants manager," declared the great umpire Bill Klem. When McGraw quit, it wasn't for health reasons as the cover-up stories said. The truth was that the Giants front office finally got fed up with his endless arrogance, bickering, and plain bad manners.

He slugged umpire Bill Byron. He nailed umpire Bob Emslie with a baseball. For years, he verbally abused Klem. And once, he threw Hank O'Day's clothes out of the umpire's dressing room and told him to return to his hotel room in his drawers.

McGraw publicly cursed National League president John Heydler. When Heydler fined McGraw for threatening an umpire in 1931, McGraw ambushed Heydler outside the St. Louis ball park and began swearing at him. When fans encircled them, McGraw cursed the fans, too.

McGraw often ended arguments with a sucker punch, and friendships with a tongue-lashing. After the Giants lost the 1913 World Series, McGraw summoned his coach, Wilbert Robinson, a close and loyal friend for 20 years, and said imperiously, "You're fired."

Considering McGraw's wrath, Robbie got off lucky. Not so fortunate was another friend, William Boyd, the actor who later portrayed cowboy hero Hopalong Cassidy. While carousing together in New York in the wee hours of August 8, 1920, Boyd objected to McGraw's vile language in the presence of a cleaning lady at the Lambs Club. McGraw responded by cracking Boyd over the head with a water pitcher.

Nothing was sacred when McGraw unleashed his tongue. Bill Klem once said, "The fellow who wrote, 'Sticks and stones may break my bones, but names can never harm me' never heard John McGraw." McGraw was so mean he once called fellow hothead Ty Cobb a "yellow-gutted, cotton'-pickin' cheat"—and got away with it.

McGraw loved to attack opposing pitchers best—by showering them with low-blow insults. Once, during a game in Philadelphia, Phillies pitcher Ad Brennan decided he had heard enough slurs from the obnoxious Giants manager. Brennan called time, left the mound, walked coolly over to the Giants dugout, and coldcocked McGraw with one punch. In gratitude, fans the next day presented Brennan with a huge bouquet of flowers.

George Brace Photo

Earl Torgeson

First Baseman • Boston-Philadelphia, N.L.;
Detroit-Chicago-New York, A.L. • 1947–61

Earl Torgeson gave baseball a new definition for the term slugger. He fought anybody, anywhere, anytime.

All a player had to do was look at him the wrong way and Torgy's fists flew into action. The tall, powerful brawler backed up his temper with the meanest left jab in the bigs. No one fooled with him—unless they were suicidal.

Torgeson led the league in emptying benches and littering the field with bodies. His baseball career read like a police rap sheet—an estimated 50 fist fights, 25 torn uniforms, and an untold number of fractures, lacerations, and bruises.

"There was always someone who wanted to clean my clock," he once complained. But who dared?

Torgeson even beat up players he admired. During a Red Sox-Braves exhibition series in Boston in 1948, Red Sox runner Billy Hitchcock grabbed Torgy's leg so the first sacker couldn't retrieve an overthrow. Torgeson proceeded to thrash Hitchcock, for which Torgy received a $100 fine from Commissioner Happy Chandler. Torgeson admitted to the commissioner that he started the fight and then commended Hitchcock for his actions. "I'd have done the same thing if I'd been in Hitchcock's place."

As a Boston Brave, Torgeson threw his cheapest and most notorious punch when he sneaked up from behind and decked his unsuspecting victim in a game against the New York Giants on July 1, 1952.

For several prior games, Torgy had been feuding with Giants catcher Sal Yvars, accusing him of setting up too close to the plate. Torgeson told the catcher to back off, but Yvars stood his ground. So whenever Torgy hit the ball, he tossed his bat back, trying to plant several bruises on Yvars. After a couple of nicks from the timber, Yvars warned Torgeson that the next time he pulled that stunt, Yvars would break Torgy's bat.

The next night, when Torgeson singled in the bottom of the first inning, his bat "accidently" hit the catcher. As promised, Yvars picked up the bat and whacked it against home plate until he split the handle.

Torgeson, not a quick thinker, stewed over this development until the bottom of the second inning. Then he strolled into the Braves dugout, took off his cap, and carefully set aside his glasses. He trotted out of the dugout and broke into a run across the diamond. By the time he reached the Giants bench, he was a charging bull with the unknowing Yvars dead in his sights.

Yvars, strapping on his catching gear, had his back turned when the Boston tough guy leaped into the dugout. Torgy didn't say a word. He just wheeled Yvars around and smashed him in the face. Yvars went straight down and Torgy, still swinging, jumped on top of him. Since the attack erupted in the New York dugout, the Giants were able to pull the furious Torgy off Yvars, saving the catcher from a more savage beating. After completing the game, Yvars went to the hospital for stitches above his eye.

National League president Warren Giles fined Torgy and called the attack "unsportsmanlike" and "repugnant."

Actually, Torgeson should have thanked Yvars for breaking his bat. With it, Torgy was hitting only .217.

Burleigh Grimes

Pitcher • Pittsburgh-Brooklyn-New York-Boston-St. Louis-Chicago, N.L. • 1916–34

Burleigh Grimes didn't belong in ball games; he belonged in horror movies. He should have been a teammate of Lon Chaney and Bela Lugosi.

Batters trembled just looking at Grimes. He didn't shave before games, so thick stubble blackened his glowering face. He often curled his upper lip in a snarl that bared yellow fangs.

He hungered to fight and he hungered to pitch and when he could do both together so much the better. Ol' Stubblebeard, who learned to throw a spitter and a duster before he was old enough to grow whiskers, was happiest when he made batters eat dirt.

Grimes was so mean he once threw a beanball at the on-deck hitter! It happened during the last days of his 19-year career, proving he was just as ferocious at the end as he was in his rookie season. Detroit's Goose Goslin had hit a homer off Grimes, so, a few innings later, the angry pitcher squared accounts. When Goose was still in the on-deck circle, the terrible-tempered Grimes low-bridged him with a blazing fastball. "Goose was so eager to get back up there and bat that he was inching out of the batter's circle," Grimes explained later. "So I let him have it."

Grimes didn't want to scare batters—he wanted to hurt them. He liked to throw at the feet of Giants first baseman Bill Terry. Years later, Terry asked him why. Grimes replied, "You hit with your feet so close together that you couldn't move them as fast as you could your head."

For years, Grimes held a deep-seated grudge against Giants second baseman Frankie Frisch, mainly because the Fordham Flash belted Grimes's pitches as if they were batting practice tosses. So almost every time the situation permitted, the vengeful Grimes sent Frisch sprawling in the dirt.

Early in the 1926 season, in a game against the Giants at Ebbets Field, Grimes fired four straight pitches at Frisch's head, driving him to the ground. The New York bench heaped a torrent of verbal abuse at the pitcher, and he retorted in kind. Then he challenged the Giants' burly

catcher, Pancho Snyder, to a fight under the stands after the game. Their post-game battle ignited a free-for-all between the two clubs.

After enough dustings for Frisch to consider opening up his own cleaning shop, he took revenge. The next time he faced Grimes, Frisch bunted down the first base line. When the pitcher fielded the ball, Frisch deliberately spiked him, nearly severing an Achilles tendon.

Months later, when Grimes was able to resume pitching, Frisch said he was sorry, that he hadn't meant to hurt Grimes so badly. But the first time Frisch faced his nemesis since the spiking, Grimes' pitch hit him squarely between the shoulder blades. "Dammit, Burleigh," moaned Frisch, wobbling painfully to first base. "I apologized."

"Yes," said Grimes sweetly, "but you didn't smile."

Dolf Luque

Pitcher • Boston-Cincinnati-Brooklyn-New York, N.L. • 1914–35

When Dolf Luque stood on the pitcher's mound, his blue eyes blazed malevolently at each hitter. He had a mean curveball and an even meaner disposition.

Hitters would rather take their chances with a firing squad than bat against Luque. They knew if they crowded the plate—which was the only way to hit his wicked curve—he'd bean their heads, crack their ribs, or smash their elbows with his "purpose" pitch. He never hit a batter by accident. He had pinpoint control of his pitches and no control of his temper. So when a batter was drilled by a pitch, it was because Luque intended to hurt him.

God forbid if a player clobbered a Luque pitch for an extra-base hit. Once, New York Giant second baseman Frankie Frisch smacked a booming triple and Luque chased him around the bases, yelling, "Next time you go down! Next time you go down!" Sure enough, Frisch hit the dirt in his next at-bat.

Cuban-born Luque, "The Pride of Havana," took guff from no one. A Cincinnati teammate barely escaped with his life after he uttered an insulting remark about Luque's Latin ancestry. Luque wasted no time getting even. He didn't bother throwing a punch or a baseball at his transgressor. Instead, Luque flung a deadly ice pick that barely missed the offender.

Bench jockeys risked their lives when they tried to ride Luque. Once, during a Cincy home game against New York in 1922, the Giant bench warmers launched a tirade of savage slurs at Luque while he pitched. The Giants shouted words that no descendant of the Spanish *grandees* could endure.

So Luque took off his glove, placed the ball in it, and carefully laid it on the mound. Then he walked over to the Giant dugout—and punched outfielder Casey Stengel in the face. The problem was that Luque had socked the wrong guy. His chief tormentor had been outfielder Bill Cunningham, who was seated next to Stengel.

Naturally, the punch sparked a wild free-for-all between the two clubs. When the dust settled, Luque was thrown out of the game. As play was about to resume, Luque suddenly reappeared in the New York dugout, bat in hand, intent on decapitating each Giant one by one. It took four policemen to subdue Luque and drag him, struggling and screaming, out of the ball park.

BOOING THE BOO BIRDS

The Most Unruly Behavior of Fans

Fans come to the ball park to watch a game and engage in one of America's favorite pastimes—booing. At the ump, the gopher-ball pitcher, the slumping slugger. But sometimes the real boos shouldn't be directed at the playing field, but right up to the stands, where fans have displayed some of the rudest, raunchiest, rowdiest behavior this side of a riot zone. For "The Most Unruly Behavior of Fans," The Baseball Hall of SHAME inducts the following:

The Kessler Brothers

Athletics Fans • 1932

One was born with a bullhorn for a throat and the other with a 78 rpm phonograph for a mouth.

They were the Kessler Brothers, Bull and Eddie. They sat on opposite sides of the diamond in old Shibe Park, and together they drove Philadelphia A's manager Connie Mack out of his mind and A's third baseman Jimmy Dykes out of town.

The Kesslers were the first to turn a Philadelphia tradition—verbally abusing the home team—into an art form. Whenever the A's were home, the Kesslers, who worked on the docks in the morning, tuned up their astonishingly loud voices and aimed their vitriolic raps at the players.

For some strange reason, they unmercifully harassed Jimmy Dykes. From their seats opposite each other, Bull and Eddie loudly debated Dykes's ability on the field and questioned the circumstances of his birth for all to hear. Their nonstop slams made Dykes dread home stands.

Whenever he bobbled a grounder, the Kesslers hooted and hollered. "The little round man missed another one!" they announced to most of Philadelphia and part of New Jersey. Whenever Dykes fanned, Bull bellowed from his first base seat, "Who always strikes out with men on base?" Replied Eddie from his third base seat, "Stand up, Jimmy Dykes!"

At times the torrent of abuse got to the normally unflappable infielder and he booted easy balls. With games at stake, Connie Mack tried everything to shut up the booming tongue-lashers. He pleaded. He cajoled. He threatened. He even bribed them with season passes.

For a while, that worked. But after a few games, the Kesslers couldn't stand the sounds of silence any longer. They turned in their passes and turned on their mouths.

In desperation, Mack hauled the Kesslers into court and sought an injunction to muzzle them. But the judge threw the request out quicker than a Walter Johnson fastball.

Finally, when Dykes no longer could take any more of "The Bull and Eddie Show," Mack was left with two choices—cut off Dykes's ears or get rid of him. At the end of the season, Dykes was sold to the Chicago White Sox.

Without their favorite target to abuse, baseball was no longer fun for the Kesslers, and they faded away, quietly.

Bleacher Creatures

Tigers Fans • 1985

The Bleacher Creatures—the 10,000 rowdy fans who sit in the cheap seats at Tiger Stadium—sank to a new low in crudeness early in the 1985 season.

Their obnoxious behavior began on a somewhat innocent note during a home game. In a mass imitation of the popular Miller Lite beer commercials, half of the bleacherites stood up and yelled, "Less filling!" while the other half responded with "Tastes great!"

But a few games later, they decided to change the words. To fans in the box seats on the other side of the field, it sounded as though half the Bleacher Creatures were shouting, "Fun cue!" and the other half replying with "Eats hit!" However, spectators in the rest of the ball park knew exactly what the Bleacher Creatures were uttering—a chant that fit their gutter mentality.

Game after game, they shouted their obscene phrases. Finally, during a night game on May 4, the public address announcer made a request that they stop the profane chant. The Bleacher Creatures responded by standing up and bowing toward home plate. But they refused to shut up.

Tigers president Jim Campbell had heard enough, and closed down the bleachers for a month. It was the second time in five years that the Bleacher Creatures were muzzled. In 1980, Campbell had blocked off the section for one day because the fans there had been disrupting games by throwing debris and beach balls onto the field. But that was a G-rated antic compared to their R-rated version of the Miller Lite commercial.

"No man or woman should have to come to the park and listen to that," fumed Detroit manager Sparky Anderson. "I can't for the life of me understand why anybody would want to chant that. I've never heard that in any other park in America." That's because no other park has the Bleacher Creatures.

Right Field Boston Fans

May 15, 1894

When the rowdies in the bleachers at Boston's South End Grounds tried to light a fire under the home team, they ended up burning down most of the hometown instead.

The 3,500 fans were getting hot under the collar during a bitter game against the visiting Baltimore Orioles, who had whomped the Beaneaters badly the day before.

In the third inning, Oriole third baseman John McGraw sent the hostile crowd into a frenzy when he started a fist fight with local hero and first baseman Tommy "Foghorn" Tucker.

While Mugsy and Foghorn traded punches, a gang of hoodlums decided to inflame the passions of fans and their team by setting a small fire in the 25-cent seats in right field. Almost everyone laughed at the prank, but it soon was no laughing matter.

When the flames began to spread in the bleachers, the umpire halted the game. Rather than leave, the fans in the grandstands became infuriated that such a small fire should stop play. Impatiently they shouted, "Play ball! Play ball!"

The players ran out to right field to help fight the fire, but once they felt the heat of the raging flames, they hightailed it for the clubhouse, cleaned out their lockers, and got the hell out of the neighborhood.

With the speed of a prairie fire, the flames engulfed the grandstand and jumped across the street, devouring block after block. Three hours after the right field idiots torched the ball park, the fire had wiped out 12 acres of the South End, including more than 170 homes, schools, churches, stores, stables, and warehouses. Fortunately, no one was killed. Unfortunately, the fire-starters got away.

Chicago Cubs Fans

July 4, 1900

Thousands of gunslinging Chicago Cubs fans turned a Fourth of July doubleheader into a shootout at the OK Corral, endangering the lives of players and fellow spectators.

Bullets sang, darted, and whizzed over the players' heads as the rambunctious fans fired round after round whenever the Cubs scored against the gun-shy Philadelphia Phillies. The visiting team was so intimidated it lost both games of the twin bill at Chicago's West Side Grounds.

In the sixth inning of the opener, the Cubs triggered an explosive six-run rally as guns and firecrackers blasted away from all sides of the ball park. When the inning finally ended, the shell-shocked Philly outfielders emerged from a haze of gunpowder smoke that hung over the field like a battleground pall.

In the second game, the Cubs tied the score in the bottom of the ninth as the fans cheered them on with a blaze of gunfire. First, the left field bleachers let loose with a salvo. Then the right field bleachers responded. Hundreds of spectators in the grandstand were so happy they began shooting holes in the roof, causing flying splinters to shower down on their heads.

By the bottom of the twelfth inning, ammunition was running short for many fans, so they pounded their seats with the butts of their guns. But others, who were still well-supplied with bullets, fired a fusillade to rattle Phils hurler Al Orth and his teammates.

The barrage worked. Philadelphia misplayed two balls for an error and an infield hit. The strain began to show on Orth. Barry McCormick laid down a sacrifice bunt that was fielded by Orth. But the nettled Orth threw wildly past first, allowing the winning run to score.

When the Cubs won, one armed-to-the-teeth fan stood up and shouted to his cohorts, "Load! Load at will! Fire!" And they did. The last remaining ammo was spent in one booming volley.

Said *The Daily Inter Ocean*, one of Chicago's major newspapers: "The actions of the spectators and the noise of the revolver shots reminded one of a pleasant little afternoon—at a lynching bee."

Tortilla Tossers

Angels Fans • 1984

The old-fashioned food fight took on a new form at Anaheim Stadium—the Tortilla Wars.

In the summer of 1984, fans in the $2.50 upper deck seats began throwing tortillas around like Frisbees during the seventh inning stretch at California Angels games. But the tossers' fling with the Mexican staff of life got out of control when several of the edible floppy disks smacked into the faces of unamused spectators. Other tortillas wound up on the playing field.

In a police crackdown during a June game, 20 tortilla tossers were kicked out of the stadium. But the food flingers continued to make tortillas at home and smuggle them into the stadium to throw. Tosser Richard

Sheratt, 24, said he used corn tortillas because they were cheaper and flew better than ones made of flour.

During the height of the Tortilla Wars, Sheratt told reporters, "The police are doing their best to suppress it, but it's gotten so big that everybody is willing to take the risk of being thrown out. We throw tortillas because it's something to do, something different. Older people used to get offended by it, but now they're doing it too."

When the rowdies weren't flinging the *platillos sabrosos*, they were dumping beer from the upper deck onto the spectators below. But the Anaheim City Council put an end to that practice, as well as the Tortilla Wars, by passing an ordinance prohibiting the throwing of foods. Fans caught in the act now face a fine up to $1,000.

At least the fad wasn't as disgusting as one seen earlier in the year. "For a while," said Anaheim police sergeant Bill Donohue, "some guy sat up there in the upper deck and ate big moths."

Frank Germano

Dodgers Fan • Sept. 16, 1940

The cry of "Kill the umpire!" is as old as baseball itself. Fans don't really mean it, although some act as if they do.

New York Daily News Photo

After the last out was made in a 4–3 Dodger loss to the Cincinnati Reds at Ebbets Field, irate fan Frank Germano jumped down on the field and wrestled burly, six-foot-four-inch umpire George Magerkurth to the ground.

Everyone was shocked when the snarling little squirt, half the size of the mighty Mage, landed several good punches. In the confusion, fellow ump Bill Stewart caught a kick in the head that opened up a gash. The only bruises Magerkurth suffered were to his ego.

Germano, 21, was arrested, and at the arraignment Magerkurth learned the punk was on parole for a petty larceny conviction. The big-hearted ump compassionately withdrew the complaint, explaining, "I'm the father of a boy myself." He shouldn't have been so forgiving.

A few years later, Germano appeared before Brooklyn Judge Samuel Liebowitz on a pickpocketing charge. Remembering him from the day of the Magerkurth assault, the judge asked, "How did you come to lose your head that day? Were you really all that stirred up because the Dodgers lost the game?"

"I was pretty stirred up," Germano said. "I was mad enough to slug Magerkurth, all right. The Dodgers shoulda won easy." He lowered his voice as he added, "But just between you and me, Judge, I had a partner in the stands that day. We wuz doin' a little business."

The little bum was just creating a disturbance so his partner could pick a few pockets.

Charles Hewes   Robert Reza
Robert Algarin

Angels Fans • July 5, 1985

Rather than direct their verbal assaults at the visiting Red Sox, these three bullies taunted the family and friends of Boston outfielder Rick Miller. But when they went too far, they triggered a wild fracas involving fans, players, and cops.

Miller's wife Janet, their 5-year-old son Joshua, and three family friends were sitting behind the Red Sox dugout in Anaheim Stadium during a night game against the Angels. According to police, the three obnoxious fans leaned over the dugout and shouted insults at the players. John Baker, 37, a friend of Miller's, asked the loudmouths to cool it out of consideration for the player's family.

The troublemaking trio became just plain mean and turned their abusive attention to Miller's family and friends. When words triggered a fist fight, Miller leaped into the stands to protect his family and rescue his friend Baker, who was outnumbered and locked in a stranglehold. Several Red Sox players and ten policemen jumped into the melee, which briefly delayed the eighth inning of the game won by the Angels 13–4.

After officers restored order, the three thugs, all from Whittier, California, were hauled off to jail. Charles Hewes, 21, and Robert Reza, 25, were booked on investigation of felonious aggravated assault of a police officer and on a misdemeanor assault. Robert Algarin, 22, was booked on investigation of interfering with a police officer and disturbing the peace.

John Baker was treated for a gash on his head, and Officer Richard Raulston was hospitalized for a separated shoulder he suffered when he was knocked down in the skirmish.

Immediately after the fight, Miller, carrying his sobbing son, led his terrified wife and friends down through the Red Sox dugout and into the safety of the Boston clubhouse.

"There was no way I could watch," said Miller after the game. "All I know is my wife was really shaken up and my son was crying."

Declared Angel third baseman Doug DeCinces, "If I was Miller, I would have done the same thing. You can take abuse, but not your family. I'm just sorry Rick didn't get the guys onto the field." Presumably, the players then would have personally pounded some sense into the three rowdies.

HEAVE HO-HO'S

The Most Inglorious Ejections from a Game

Although umpires don't see all the things they should, they usually manage to hear all the things they shouldn't. What usually follows is a heated argument that often ends when the arbiter thumbs his antagonist out of the game. However, this ritual sometimes takes a bizarre twist and ends up looking like a Barnum & Bailey sideshow. For "The Most Inglorious Ejections from a Game," The Baseball Hall of SHAME inducts the following:

The Voice

July 19, 1946

A mysterious ventriloquist whose heckling from the stands sounded as if it was coming from the dugout caused the ejections of 14 innocent Chicago White Sox players.

The Voice baffled umpire Red Jones and instigated one of the biggest mass evictions in baseball history.

Jones was working behind the plate in Boston when he reprimanded Chicago pitcher Joe Haynes for allegedly throwing a beanball at Ted Williams. Then the ventriloquist went into action.

When Jones heard one too many barbs coming from what he thought was the dugout, he threw out Ralph Hodgin, one of the quietest players on the team. But The Voice would not be silenced, and players joined in the heckling. Three more White Sox were tossed out. Nevertheless, The Voice kept hollering insults from the shadows of the dugout, so the beleaguered arbiter ejected his fifth player of the day. Still, there was no relief for Jones.

The bench jockeying, led by The Voice, had driven the now frantic umpire over the edge. In frustration, Jones ordered the entire bench cleared of the nine remaining players and coaches. As the nine paraded from their third base dugout to the clubhouse runway on the first base side, each had some choice things to say to the tormented umpire.

"Take these," said coach Bing Miller, offering his glasses to Jones. "You need 'em more than I do."

With an empty Chicago dugout, Jones was free of harassment. Or so he thought. Suddenly, Jones heard, "Hey, meathead, let's see some hustle before the home folks!" It was The Voice.

Earl Weaver

Manager • Baltimore, A.L. • Sept. 29, 1985

Managers Mel Ott, Billy Martin, and Earl Weaver have all received the old heave-ho twice in a doubleheader. But only the hotheaded Weaver was given his second thumb of the day *before* the start of the nightcap.

The ejections were the 92nd and 93rd in the ruckus-raising career of the fiesty Baltimore Orioles skipper.

Weaver went on the warpath in the first inning of the first game of a doubleheader at Yankee Stadium. For ten minutes, he quarreled with plate umpire Nick Bremigan over a foul ball. In the second inning, Weaver launched into a seven-minute tirade over a dropped third strike.

When the quick-tempered manager charged out of the dugout in the third inning to question a decision, Bremigan had seen more than enough of Weaver. "You're gone!" the ump shouted. "You've been out here too much today."

New York Daily News Photo

But Weaver refused to leave the field. Umpiring crew chief Jim Evans pulled out a stopwatch and told Weaver, "You're wasting time." The fuming manager grabbed the watch and hurled it into the Orioles dugout. "I would have thrown the watch into the stands if I had a better arm," said Weaver. "But my arm isn't what it used to be."

As Weaver stalked off the field, one of the umpires yelled at him, "Go back home and play golf, Earl. The game has passed you by."

After sulking in the clubhouse for the rest of the game, the "Earl of Baltimore" was still spitting fire when he delivered the lineup card before the start of the second game. At home plate, he confronted Evans and told him that after the first-game ejection, Orioles second baseman Rich Dauer had heard the ump say, "I want to meet Weaver in the parking lot after the game." (Presumably, it was to discuss baseball—with his fists.)

Evans denied he had ever made such a threat. Then, in a voice rising in anger with every word, Evans snarled at Weaver, "You're free to go out to the parking lot right now, 'cause you're outta here!" For the second time that day, Weaver got the boot.

To cap off this history-making event, Weaver kicked dirt on Evans, then scooped up a big handful of dirt and threw it at the umpire. Because of

Weaver's childish outbursts, he was suspended for three days—the sixth suspension of his career.

This wasn't the first time that Weaver had been ejected twice in one day. In a doubleheader on August 15, 1975, the bickering manager was thumbed out by umpire Ron Luciano during the first game and then again before the start of the nightcap.

"Weaver is like a nightmare that keeps coming back," declared Nick Bremigan. "To me, he is the Ayatollah of the eighties."

Tom Gorman

Umpire • July 1, 1963

National League umpire Tom Gorman deserves the thumb—for knowingly throwing out the wrong player.

Gorman was calling balls and strikes in a game in Philadelphia when one of the Phillies started blasting the ump from the dugout with remarks such as "Where's your Seeing Eye dog?" and "Why don't you punch a hole in your mask?" The tormentor wouldn't let up and, by the seventh inning, Gorman had taken enough guff.

The ump decided to take a shot at somebody, so he figured he'd toss out third baseman Don Hoak, who had had a run-in with him the previous week. Besides, it wouldn't hurt the team much, reasoned Gorman, because Hoak had a leg injury and wasn't even playing.

Pointing toward the corner of the dugout where he thought he spotted Hoak, Gorman shouted, "Okay, Hoak, you're out of there!"

Philly manager Gene Mauch rushed to the plate in protest. "Why are you picking on my ball players? So far you've been working a pretty good game, not bad for you. You've only missed six or seven pitches so far."

"Don't play around with me," said Gorman. "Get that donkey Hoak out of the dugout."

Mauch put his hands on his hips and pushed his face to within inches of the umpire's. "Let me tell you something," snapped Mauch. "Hoak isn't in the dugout. He's in the bull pen." The bull pen was 380 feet away. "What are you going to do now?"

Trying hard not to turn red from embarrassment, Gorman replied, "Get him over here."

Mauch waved to the bull pen and Hoak jogged in, thinking he was going to pinch-hit. When Mauch told him, "Gorman just put you out," Hoak started ranting and raving and jumping up and down. But Gorman would not be swayed. He tossed Hoak out.

The next day, Hoak bumped into Gorman in the clubhouse runway leading to the field. "Answer me one thing, Tom," said Hoak. "How the hell did you know I was hollering down in the bull pen?"

Doug Zimmer   Al Friedman

Cameramen • Sports Channel • May 9, 1984

Sports Channel cable TV cameramen Doug Zimmer and Al Friedman proved that television has no place in the dugout.

They were booted out of a game by umpire Joe West because, in a rank breach of broadcasting confidence, they showed a controversial replay to several players during a game.

Zimmer and Friedman, who were covering the Mets-Braves game at Shea Stadium, edged down to the corner of the New York dugout to get better shots for the viewers. From that vantage point, the cameramen followed Met baserunner Hubie Brooks as he tried to score from second base on a single in the fourth inning. West called Brooks out at the plate.

Manager Davey Johnson, incensed by the call, argued vehemently with West, but to no avail. Meanwhile, coach Bobby Valentine and pitcher Mike Torrez huddled in front of the Sports Channel camera monitor in the dugout as Zimmer and Friedman showed an instant replay of the action.

What the Mets saw enraged them even more. They loudly let West know that he'd blown the play. In return, West let the two TV cameramen know they had blown their welcome. In a move guaranteed not to win him any Emmys, West threw Zimmer and Friedman out of the game.

The next day, the Mets management called National League president Chub Feeney to complain about West's thumb. Feeney explained that although the ejections were without precedent, it's against the rules to show replays to players on the bench. West was right in pulling the plug on the TV boys.

RAZING THE ROOF

The Worst Ball Parks for Watching and Playing Games

The unimaginative, circular, all-purpose stadiums now dominating the game are definitely drab and impersonal. They're nothing like the ball parks erected before domes, artificial turf, and theater seats. The old structures had style, color, and charm. Oh yeah? Many are just as bad as the new ones. Some were built by people who must have hated baseball, because inside these monstrosities fans and players alike have frozen and fried and risked life and limb. For "The Worst Ball Parks for Watching and Playing Games," The Baseball Hall of SHAME inducts the following:

Fenway Park

Boston • 1912–present

Fenway is a nice place to visit, but you wouldn't want to play there. Teams don't just battle each other; they must fight the sun, the wind, the fog, the pigeons, and the Green Monster.

This innocent-looking stadium boasts one of the most intimidating sun fields in baseball. It is said in Boston that the sun rises in the east and sets in the eyes of the right fielder.

Actually, the sun blinds everybody. In late September, 1972, the Red Sox started an important game against Detroit by losing in the sun the first two fly balls the Tigers hit. That same year, a high hopper hit Chicago White Sox pitcher Wilbur Wood in the knee because he was blinded by the sun.

Weather at Fenway is like George Steinbrenner on a bad day—totally unpredictable. New England gale winds have not only blown pop flies into homers but also torn the big hand from the old center field clock and bent the left field foul pole. On April 25, 1962, the blustery east wind dropped the temperature at Fenway from 78 degrees to 58 degrees in 10 minutes.

When the winds die down, the fog often rolls in as thick as clam chowder. On August 8, 1966, the game had to be stopped four times because of poor visibility.

Mother Nature abuses players in other ways. She gives pigeons and seagulls one-way tickets to Fenway. On May 17, 1947, St. Louis Browns hurler Ellis Kinder was bombed when a seagull dropped a three-ounce smelt on the mound.

But pigeons are Fenway's national bird. Detroit slugger Willie Horton mortally wounded a pigeon with a foul fly near home plate in April 1974. In 1945, a Fenway pigeon got in the way of a throw from Athletics outfielder Hal Peck on a double by Boston's Skeeter Newsome. The pigeon lost some feathers. The A's lost the game.

That same season, Boston outfielder Tom McBride took a bead on what he felt sure was a long fly off the bat of Philadelphia's Sam Chapman. Too late McBride discovered his error—he had been chasing a pigeon.

(If Ted Williams had had his way, there would have been few pigeons to squawk about. After a game in 1940, he grabbed a shotgun and blasted about 40 of the dirty birds out of the sky. But then the Humane Society swooped down on him with a severe reprimand.)

The weather and the birds haven't influenced the way baseball is played at Fenway as much as the Green Monster has. The 37-foot-high wall, topped by a 23-foot-high screen, looms a mere 315 feet from the plate to the left field foul pole.

A routine fly in most other parks—just a nice lazy can of corn—can magically turn into a home run over the Fenway screen. On the other hand, rising line drives that would soar out of other parks just dent the Green Monster, going for doubles, and sometimes only singles.

The fans may like to watch games at Fenway because it's so cozy, traditional, and intimate. But unless they have especially weak bladders, the men tend to shy away from the bathrooms. That's because almost everyone who uses the trough-like urinals comes away wet.

Hubert H. Humphrey Metrodome

Minneapolis • 1982–present

"It's a travesty," said Toronto manager Bobby Cox. "Hit the ball on the ground and it bounces over your head. Hit it in the air and you can't see it."

"It's the worst place ever," declared Baltimore outfielder Fred Lynn.

"This place stinks," complained Yankee manager Billy Martin. "It's a shame it was named after a great guy like Humphrey."

Those are some of the nicer things said about the Metrodome, the indoor playground of the Minnesota Twins.

Whoever designed the Dome had a weird sense of humor. Baseballs bounce like tennis balls on the SuperTurf. High pop-ups get trapped in the low ceiling. Players lose sight of balls against the gray-white background.

Fans in the upper deck in left field get their fannies fried by the heat from the scoreboard.

It's the only stadium ever to draw an official protest. After letting two easy pop-ups drop because they couldn't see them, the Yankees played the next game at the Metrodome under protest. On May 8, 1985, manager Billy Martin charged that the Dome wasn't up to major league standards and should be banned from baseball. The protest was denied.

The fast, bouncy SuperTurf grants the Twins a Dome-court advantage. It also turns banjo hitters into sluggers. In 1984, the Twins and their opponents whacked 304 doubles and 47 triples at the Dome, compared to only 220 doubles and 16 triples in away games.

In a June 1985 game at the Dome, Twins second baseman Tim Teufel hit a simple 150-foot fly that turned into a cheap inside-the-park homer when it fell and then bounced over the head of Chicago White Sox right fielder Harold Baines.

Until adjustments were made before the 1985 All-Star Game, the lights were too bright on the right side and too dim on the left side. Complaining of glare, Twins right fielder Tom Brunansky wore sunglasses in the outfield, a bizarre sight in an indoor stadium.

Blue Jays shortstop Alfredo Griffin lost a hopper over the mound in the lights, which prompted his coach Bob Didier to say, "Only in Minnesota could someone lose a ground ball in the lights during the day."

The low ceiling has created some high drama. In a game against Oakland on May 4, 1984, A's slugger Dave Kingman hit a sky-high pop-up over the pitcher's mound. The ball never came down. It went through an eight-inch hole in the Metrodome's fabric roof about 180 feet above home plate. Kingman was awarded a ground-rule double.

From the fans' point of view, the Dome is boring, and built to stay that way. National Guard armories have more appeal than the Dome. "The idea," said a spokesman, "is to get the fans in, let 'em see a game, and then let 'em go home." To make it even more dull, the city fathers passed an ordinance against excessive noise. Thus, the Metrodome is the only stadium in the major leagues where you can get arrested for cheering too loudly.

Braves Field

Boston • 1915–52

Braves Field was destined for shame.

The infield terrorized fielders with sinkholes. The outfield antagonized batters with a playing surface large enough to be named a country.

The ball park's legacy of shame began during its construction. While converting the site from a golf course to a ball park, workers were plagued by cave-ins. In 1914, a huge cave-in buried alive a dozen horses and mules along what later became the third base line.

During one game a few years later, the shortstop area suddenly sank about eight inches, chasing a scared Rabbit Maranville to the dugout, where he stayed until the hole was filled.

For years, the outfield was so big it became a power hitter's hell and a careless pitcher's paradise. With nearly 11 acres of playing surface, Braves Field had the largest outfield area in the majors.

Upon seeing the park for the first time, Ty Cobb squinted down the incredibly long 402-foot foul lines and gazed at the out-of-sight center field fence 550 feet away and announced, "Nobody is ever going to hit one out of this place." Not until 1925, ten years after the park was opened, did anyone knock the ball over the fence.

Between the expansive outfield and the strong prevailing winds that blew in, low-scoring games were the rule. In 1928, Judge Emil Fuchs, owner of the Braves, decided to make it easier for his team to smack homers. The left and center field fences were moved in to 353 feet and 387 feet respectively. Unfortunately, the opposition hit twice as many four-baggers as did the Braves. The next year, Fuchs moved the fences back.

The ground-level scoreboard in left field also caused some havoc for the Braves. In 1916, New York Giants catcher Bill Rariden hit his only homer of the year when his drive bounced through the manual scoreboard in an opening left unattended by a careless employee. Teammate Johnny Rawlings swatted a cheap home run the same way in 1922.

In 1946, the owners spent $500,000 to revitalize the ball park and to improve goodwill among the fans. When spectators in one section left their seats after the home opener, they found their clothes daubed with green paint that had not been given enough time to dry. Ads in the daily papers expressed the Braves' apologies and requested fans with legitimate cleaning bills to submit them to the club for payment. The team paid 5,000 claimants—though more than 18,000 claims were filed, including some from as far away as California and Florida.

Jarry Park

Montreal • 1969–76

Jarry Park was the world's only bilingual outdoor insane asylum. You had to be nuts to play or attend a game there.

The bumpy infield and the rolling outfield at the Montreal Expos' first home drew the wrath of many a fielder. After one pre-game practice, Pittsburgh's Bob Robertson snidely asked, "When do they let the cows out?"

In April, when the field began to thaw, runners had to contend with rubbery base paths. Sometimes the pitching mound and the area around home plate would actually sink a few inches, forcing the groundskeepers to rebuild them quickly.

To all the players, "Canadian Sunset" was not a lovely song but a dangerous hazard. During the first two weeks of every June, the sunset blinded fielders at the start of night games. Thus, Jarry Park gave birth to "dusk doubles" and "twilight triples."

"Only here do I wear sunglasses for a night game," said Expo Ron Fairly in 1970. But the shades didn't always help the sure-handed first baseman. In the first inning of a game on June 13, 1970, Expos shortstop Bobby Wine fielded a ground ball and threw to Fairly, but the first baseman, blinded by the setting sun behind third base, never saw the throw. It sailed by his ear, and the runner ended up on second base. "The sun was so bad, I told Bobby Wine and [second baseman] Gary Sutherland they'd be better off to roll the ball to me," said Fairly.

The midday sun also bothered the players, especially in the early years. The huge lights were so clean that the sun's glare reflected off them and into the eyes of fielders. "It may be the only place where someone lost a ball in the lights during a day game," mused Expos manager Gene Mauch.

The fans suffered right along with the players. The 30,000-seat single-deck structure offered absolutely no protection from the snow, sleet, and cold rains of spring or from the hot sun in the dog days of summer.

The ball park even caused problems for people outside the stadium. Situated a few yards beyond the right field fence was a swimming pool. In addition to watching swimmers, the lifeguards had to keep an eye out for home run balls to make sure they wouldn't conk an unsuspecting swimmer on the head.

The Expos eventually moved into Olympic Stadium—and shed no tears when they bid Parc Jarry adieu.

SUBSTANDARD BEARERS

The Sorriest Role Models for America's Youth

Baseball players set examples for kids, but, unfortunately, not all examples are good ones. Imagine if youngsters emulated some of the game's most woeful "heroes," those rogues and malingerers who seem to live each day in foul territory. Kids would learn everything from spitting tobacco juice to shooting moons in public. They would avoid responsibility with excuses fit for a hypochondriac or a ne'er-do-well. For "The Sorriest Role Models for America's Youth," The Baseball Hall of SHAME inducts the following:

Rick Bosetti

Outfielder • Philadelphia-St. Louis, N.L.; Toronto-Oakland, A.L. • 1976–82

Most ball players have lofty, high-minded goals, such as hitting over .300 or winning 20 games—the kind of dreams that inspire greatness. Bosetti had a goal too, but it was related more to the sewer than the mountain top.

When he was with the Toronto Blue Jays, Bosetti set out to pee on every natural grass outfield in baseball.

"I've gotten all the American League parks," he chortled to the press in 1979. "That's why I want inter-league play. To water that beautiful grass in Wrigley Field [in Chicago] would be a dream come true."

Bosetti claimed that he wet the grass without a hose only in pre-game warm-ups when there were no fans in the park. But it was an open secret around the league that he did it during games while pitching changes were being made. He wanted to prove that he could take a leak before thousands of fans and not be noticed. He accomplished this feat by turning to the outfield wall and putting his glove in front of his waist.

He exposed his talents off the field as well. After being seated in a stuffy restaurant that had refused him service a few weeks earlier, Bosetti walked into the men's room, took off all his clothes, then marched through the dining room and out the door.

It was his way of thumbing his nose at people—only he didn't use his nose.

Steve Hamilton

Pitcher • Cleveland-Washington-New York-Chicago, A.L.; San Francisco-Chicago, N.L. • 1961–72

No self-respecting mother wanted her son to become a spitting image of Steve Hamilton.

The hurler was one of the messiest tobacco chewers and spitters in all of baseball.

"I spray my shots and brown streams flow down my chin," he once confessed to reporters. "It almost cost me my marriage. Once I was trying to show off in front of my wife and I spat on her open-toed shoes. She wouldn't speak to me for weeks."

Hamilton, a raw-boned Kentuckian who had his first "chaw" at the age of three, refined his disgusting habit through 12 years in the major leagues and was recognized by the Smokeless Tobacco Council as the champion tobacco chewer and spitter in baseball.

But no matter how hard he tried to live up to his fellow chewers' expectorations, he faced the ultimate embarrassment once when he lost his chaw—and his lunch—on the mound. While pitching for the Yankees on a brutally hot day in Kansas City, Hamilton threw a fastball so hard that he accidentally swallowed his chaw. He turned his back to the plate and retched. Though he had long ago survived the tobacco virility rights that have corroded the palates of thousands of pubescent American males, Hamilton was forced to leave the game green-gilled and woozy.

Nevertheless, Hamilton, with his ever-present baseball-sized wad jammed in his cheek, promoted chewing tobacco wherever he went, much to the dismay of mothers everywhere.

While most pitchers had a book on every hitter in the league, Hamilton carried a book on every tobacco spitter in the league. He knew the sprayers, the line-drive spitters, and the finesse boys. He even had a tobacco atlas that listed the distances between cities, not in miles, but in chews. For example, Chicago is about five chews from Cincinnati.

Hamilton scoffed at players who mixed tobacco with bubble gum. "Why, that's like putting fox tails on a Mercedes," he said. "No purist would think of such a thing. It's downright dishonest."

Hamilton said he admired his manager, Ralph Houk of the Yankees, because Houk liked to sneak up behind an unsuspecting, preoccupied player and shoot a squirt of tobacco juice into his back pocket.

But Hamilton's greatest hero was Les Peden, a successful minor league manager. "Old Les would chew all day and take the wad out and put it on the dresser at night, renewing it the next day," said Hamilton. "He never took it out when he ate, drank, or talked. He was a master."

New York Yankees

Aug. 1, 1979

After refusing to sign autographs for pleading youngsters, the Yankees reached the bottom—literally. Ignoring their young fans, the players delightedly signed autographs on the rear end of a luscious blonde who had dropped her jeans.

The bare facts were revealed by the mother of a 9-year-old boy. Outside Comiskey Park following a Yankee-White Sox game, the boy was seeking autographs at the same time as the sexy groupie.

His mother, Rosemary Glynn, of Orland Park, Illinois, complained that after her son and others were refused autographs, "this blonde girl, about 20 years old and pretty, walked up and they let her on the [Yankees] bus. I couldn't believe it. They wouldn't give autographs to any of the kids, but they were signing their names to that girl's bare butt."

In recounting the incident to Chicago columnist Mike Royko, Mrs.

Glynn said that the young woman then got off the bus, followed by Yankee manager Billy Martin. He asked the woman if he could photograph her, and the woman then pulled down her pants for him. "Well, I thought my little boy's eyes were going to pop out of his head," declared Mrs. Glynn.

She said the players started cheering and banging on the bus windows, and that the woman responded by wiggling her buns.

The Yankee front office tried to get to the bottom of the incident but then decided to put the whole matter behind them.

Dave Kingman

Outfielder-First baseman-Designated Hitter • **San Francisco-New York-San Diego-Chicago, N.L.; California-New York-Oakland, A.L.** • **1971-present**

Few players have shown such disdain for their teams or their fans as has Dave Kingman.

Each time he joined a team—he's been on seven clubs in 14 years—the fans wanted to give him their love and the owners wanted to give him their money. In return, he ignored the fans and bad-mouthed the owners. Teammates counted on his moral and hitting support. Sportswriters counted on his insights and quotes. He proved he was no team player and no sportswriter's friend.

Nowhere did Kingman operate more as a law unto himself than in Chicago. After he played for four different teams in one year and earned a label as a malcontent, the Cubs, fans, and press greeted him with open arms when he joined the team in 1978.

Yet by 1980, Kingman had squandered it all. His admirers soon saw him for what he was—a spoiled brat who hid in a hero's uniform.

Before a game at Wrigley Field on August 7, 1980, the Cubs gave 15,000 young fans free T-shirts bearing the image of their hero, Dave Kingman. Where was Kingman? The slugger, who had an ache in his shoulder and needed rest, shunned the ball park entirely. Instead, he showed up at a city festival where he appeared—for a fee—in a booth to promote the Jet-Ski, a marine version of a snowmobile.

Kingman was on the disabled list for six weeks, but not once did he go to the park to watch his teammates play. Since he was still collecting a large salary while on the disabled list, the least he could have done was show up at Wrigley Field to act as a dugout cheerleader. Instead, on company time, he lolled on his yacht. That's the old team spirit.

Before he was injured, Kingman had shown his lack of responsibility to the team by failing to show up for a June 13 game, which the Cubs lost. He was fined $1,250.

Even when he's nice, he's thoughtless. His teammates had gone out of their way to be kind to him. In appreciation, Kingman tossed a party for all the guys at his home. Shortly after it got started, he announced, "I have a date so I'm leaving. Here's the key. Stay as long as you like, and the last to leave be sure to lock up."

Kingman reserved most of his scorn for the press. He refused to talk to sportswriters after a spring training story quoted several Cubs, in jest, as saying he was the worst-dressed player on the team.

On April 4, 1980, he dumped a large plastic bucket full of ice and water on a sportswriter and snarled, "Now you've got something to write about for two days." A month before, he had behaved like a class A jerk while filming a TV special about himself for which he'd been paid handsomely. Kingman poured a cold beer down the back of TV producer Sandra Weir, threw her in his hot tub, and also tossed her, fully-clothed, off his yacht and into the water.

Another time, Kingman uttered a veiled threat at sportswriter Ray Sons. While taking batting practice swings before a game, Kingman said to Sons, who was nearby, "I wouldn't stand there if I were you. You might get hurt, and some people might think I did it on purpose."

Despite his hostility toward the press, Kingman wrote a weekly column for the *Chicago Tribune* in 1980. But the *Tribune* dumped Kingman for goofing off, proving the newspaper got smart quicker than the Cubs, who didn't unload him until after the 1980 season.

Jim Palmer

Pitcher • Baltimore, A.L. • 1965–84

Jim Palmer was a consistent 20-game winner, but he set a bad example by also being a consistent 20-game whiner. The Baltimore Oriole hurler suffered so many questionable ailments that Hippocrates would have turned him away.

In 1984, Palmer complained of a pinched nerve that he said he got when he was on the mound and looked over his shoulder toward first base. Weeks later, Palmer nixed a starting assignment in Minnesota, claiming he was suffering from a neck injury caused by sleeping on a hotel pillow that was too soft.

What gained him charter membership in the Pain of the Month Club was his 1984 complaint to manager Joe Altobelli: "Joe, you know what hurts most? It's my forehead, from wearing my cap during games."

Despite all his whining, Palmer didn't want to go on the disabled list because, according to his contract, he could collect an additional $50,000 by staying off the DL for the year.

Although he personifies virility and fitness by modeling in his underwear, Palmer never felt "well." He complained of pain everywhere from his trapezius muscle to his rhomboid muscle, enough ailments to provide material for a whole class of medical students. Earl Weaver marked his seasons as Orioles manager by Palmer's injuries: "There was the Year of the Back, the Year of the Shoulder, and the Year of the Ulna Nerve."

Palmer's exaggerated concern for his health bordered on the bizarre. Immediately after pitching a game, he often visited his personal physician for a late-night examination. When fellow pitcher Wayne Garland learned that he would miss the balance of the season because of a torn rotator cuff, Palmer quickly telephoned him for details. By the next afternoon, Palmer was showing the identical symptoms.

During 1979 spring training, Palmer was slowed down by a sore back. Then the back healed and the pain moved to his forearm. Next, the pain filtered to his elbow. He said he couldn't pitch. He had more excuses than a parolee caught red-handed.

Even though he fouled up the pitching rotation by his inability to pitch when he was scheduled, the Orioles put up with his pains and complaints—most of the time. On Father's Day, 1979, Weaver had enough of Palmer's bellyaching. The manager left a newspaper article about Palmer's excuses on the front of the pitcher's locker. Weaver scrawled on it, "Happy Father's Day. Now grow up!"

Bert Blyleven

Pitcher • Minnesota-Texas-Cleveland, A.L.; Pittsburgh, N.L. • 1970–present

With all of the shameful deeds he's pulled, Bert Blyleven could act as a pa-role model.

Blyleven was fined and suspended for three days for communicating his feelings to fans in Baltimore. Taken out of a game on April 28, 1985, he flipped the finger to the crowd. Then, he did it again just before stepping into the dugout.

In his final game with the Minnesota Twins in 1976, he left the mound and shot the bird to the hometown crowd, which had taunted him earlier with choruses of "Bye, Bye, Bertie" because he had demanded to be traded.

His obscene outbursts aren't the only reasons he gained entry into The Baseball Hall of SHAME. What counts most is the way he behaves off the mound.

While wearing his favorite shirt—a sport shirt with two alligators in a compromising position—he has signed autographs for his young fans. In 1982, coaching a Little League team when he was disabled with an arm injury, he taught kids how to look like major leaguers. The parents were thrilled to have Blyleven coach their children—until they discovered that he had passed out chewing tobacco to the youngsters.

Blyleven gained a reputation for being an expert on astronomy—or at least on the moon. During 1982 spring training, Cleveland sportscaster Pete Franklin was conducting a talk show in the lobby of a Tucson, Arizona hotel. Blyleven arrived, dropped his pants, and bent over. Howling with laughter, Franklin delivered a revealing play-by-play of Blyleven's antics.

Blyleven's moons have appeared day and night—even during a ball game. During spring training, Cleveland pitcher Dennis Lewallyn caught a view of Blyleven's moon down the right field line at Tucson's Hi Corbett Field. "A disgusting sight," said Lewallyn.

But what might be Blyleven's most disgusting prank took place when he was with the Pirates. Blyleven decided to make teammate John Milner toss his cookies. Blyleven mixed red gum with his chewing tobacco, sat next to Milner, faked a coughing attack and spit up what appeared to be his whole insides. Milner nearly passed out.

PITIFUL PICKOFFS

The Most Boneheaded Pickoff Victims

Sometimes, no matter how hard you try, there's just no place to hide your shame. Nobody knows this better than the base runner who's just been picked off. He brushes the dirt off the front of his uniform and, his ears ringing from the jeers of the fans, makes the long walk back into the dugout to face the sneering contempt of his teammates. For "The Most Boneheaded Pickoff Victims," The Baseball Hall of SHAME inducts the following:

Frenchy Bordagaray

Outfielder • Brooklyn, N.L. • Aug. 14, 1935

Frenchy Bordagaray had a horrible penchant for getting picked off second base—including once when he was standing on the bag!

It happened during a home game against the Cubs. After the Dodger outfielder reached second base, Brooklyn manager Casey Stengel, who was coaching at first base, held up the game and went out to talk to Bordagaray.

George Brace Photo

"Now look here, Frenchy," said Stengel. "I want you to stand on second until the batter actually hits the ball. I mean stand right on the bag. Don't take a lead, don't even move away from it six inches. Do you understand?"

"Why certainly, Mr. Stengel," Frenchy replied.

Moments later, pitcher Larry French whirled and fired a pickoff throw to second. Cubs shortstop Billy Jurges grabbed the ball and put the tag on Bordagaray for the out.

As the Frenchman passed Stengel on the way to the dugout, the disgusted manager hissed, "What were you doing out there? Weren't you standing on the bag? How could they pick you off?"

"I haven't the slightest idea, Boss," answered the bewildered Bordagaray. "I did just like you told me. I didn't move from the base even three inches. I was just standing there tapping my foot on the bag, waiting for the next batter to bang one."

"I see," said Stengel, wiping the sweat from his fevered brow. "In that case, how did Jurges manage to put you out?"

Frenchy sighed and threw up his hands in defeat. "It beats me, Boss. He must have put the tag on me between taps."

Ron LeFlore

Outfielder • Montreal, N.L. • July 28, 1980

Ron LeFlore knew that stealing a base requires concentration. But he learned the hard way that *staying* on base also requires concentration.

In a game against Cincinnati at Olympic Stadium in Montreal, LeFlore easily stole second for his 62nd theft of the year. As he stood up and brushed himself off, he noticed that the electronic scoreboard had flashed an interesting message: It was 115 years ago to the day that the first stolen base had been recorded by Ed Cuthbert.

Like many of the fans attending the game, LeFlore found this little piece of historical information fascinating. Maybe too much so. While he was standing there *reading* about baseball, he forgot about *playing* baseball—and was promptly picked off second.

Herb Washington

Designated Runner • Oakland, A.L. • Oct. 13, 1974

Herb Washington proved beyond a shadow of a doubt that the idea of a designated runner—the brainchild of A's owner Charlie Finley—was way off base.

During the 1974 World Series, Washington confirmed the belief, shared by fans and players alike, that the designated runner had no business in baseball. In front of 60 million people who were watching the Series on TV, the Dodgers picked Washington off first, snuffing out a ninth-inning rally.

Finley had plucked Washington from the college track circuit, where the speedster had run 100 meters in 10 seconds and 100 yards in 9.2. Finley had signed Washington to a contract solely as a pinch runner who would steal bases. He would never need to hold a bat or put on a glove.

Washington proudly donned his Oakland uniform for the 1974 season, but he never really got off the blocks the way Finley expected. That season and part of the next, Washington appeared in 109 games, but could show only a meager 30 career steals in 48 attempts. St. Louis Cardinals base stealer Lou Brock could do that in a good six weeks.

Finley was roundly criticized, but he patiently waited for the 1974 World Series to prove that his innovation would work. At last, Herb Washington could show the world his dazzling speed, his daring baserunning, his ability to go in there in a tight spot and win one for the A's.

His golden opportunity came in the ninth inning of the second game, with one out and the Dodgers leading 3–2. Washington, a pinch runner representing the tying run, edged away from first. Ever so carefully he widened his lead, his feet itching to sprint toward second.

A cobra ready to strike, Washington stared at pitcher Mike Marshall. Marshall, a mongoose ready to pounce, stared back. Washington stared. Marshall stared. Suddenly Marshall made his move. Washington didn't. The next sound he heard was the ball slapping into the glove of first baseman Steve Garvey. The next sensation he felt was that of getting tagged on the hand. The next thing he saw was umpire Doug Harvey's thumb in the air.

It was one of the last things he saw in the majors. Washington, the man who was born to run, was run out of baseball the following year.

Barry Bonnell   Dave Collins   Willie Upshaw
Outfielder   Outfielder   First Baseman

Toronto, A.L. • Aug. 24, 1983

In the most stunning display of sheer base-running ineptness in one inning, three Blue Jay runners reached first—and all three were picked off.

In the top of the tenth inning against the Orioles, Toronto held a 4–3 lead, with no outs and Barry Bonnell on first. Blue Jays manager Bobby Cox flashed the steal sign. After all, the Orioles had used up all their regular catchers and now had infielder Lenn Sakata behind the plate. The Blue Jays thought they could merely stroll around the bases against the inexperienced catcher.

Bonnell took his lead off first, eager to test Sakata's arm. Unfortunately, Bonnell was a little too eager. Relief pitcher Tippy Martinez whipped the ball to first and caught Bonnell flat-footed for the first out.

The next batter, Dave Collins, walked. He had a look of a man ready to take candy from a baby—but instead he got his own pocket picked. He strayed off first just enough to become pickoff victim number two.

Now it was Willie Upshaw's turn to join the pickoff parade. After getting an infield hit, he too was all set to steal off Sakata when he got picked off like the others.

Incredibly, Martinez retired the side without getting a batter out.

As if that wasn't embarrassing enough for the Blue Jays, in the bottom of the tenth, the Orioles tied the score. Then Sakata—the guy whom they were going to steal the game from—blasted a three-run homer to win the game for Baltimore, 7–4.

TURNSTILE TURNOFFS

Ball Park Promotions That Backfired

Baseball teams enjoy spreading cheer—and filling seats—by offering gimmicks, giveaways, and lots of hoopla at games. These ball park promotions are designed to give fans more than their money's worth. But sometimes these marketing schemes give teams much more than they bargained for. For "Ball Park Promotions That Backfired," The Baseball Hall of SHAME inducts the following:

Army Day

Shea Stadium • June 10, 1975

A thunderous 21-gun salute honoring the Army created some embarrassing repercussions for the New York Yankees.

Barry Landers, Yankees promotions director, decided to celebrate the U.S. Army's 200th birthday by holding "Army Day" at Shea Stadium (where the team was playing during the renovation of Yankee Stadium).

A battery from Fort Hamilton positioned two 75 mm cannons on the warning track, facing the center field flag. The Army brass assured Landers that the paraffin in the cannons would flash harmlessly and burn out after flying about 20 feet over the fence and onto a grassy area beyond. The Army experts were probably the same ones who predicted the Vietnam War would last only a few months.

With an ear-splitting boom, the battery fired the first salute—and knocked down part of the fence. But rather than call a cease-fire, the soldier boys kept right on blasting away. The whole stadium filled with smoke and shook with earthquake force. Glass shattered in the stadium's exclusive enclosed Diamond Club, adding to the terror.

When the smoke cleared, 31,809 temporarily deaf fans saw a gaping hole in the center field fence. The cannoneers had blown away three fence panels and set fire to a fourth. The fire was quickly doused. The game was delayed while groundskeepers hurriedly covered the holes with plywood.

"I was the one who got the idea," said a chagrined Landers. "I was the one who got the blame, too." He also was the one who ended up with the nickname "Boom-Boom."

Commenting on the promotion on his nightly newscast, Walter Cronkite told his viewers, "I never give sports scores. But I cannot resist this one. The score in New York was Army 21, Fence 0."

Fan Appreciation Day

Yankee Stadium • Oct. 2, 1982

The New York Yankees had a rather peculiar way of celebrating "Fan Appreciation Day"—they beat up two of their fans.

Spectators Dennis Denbeck, 32, of Long Island City, New York, and Joe Turnbull, 32, of Bergenfield, New Jersey, were singled out for special treatment after they put brown paper bags over their heads in a harmless, comic protest over New York's dismal fifth-place finish.

According to witnesses, the men, their wives, and their friends had finished singing "Take Me Out To The Ball Game" during the seventh-inning stretch when two security cops told Denbeck and Turnbull to take off their paper bags. The two refused, so the guards ordered the whole group to leave.

When they wouldn't budge, one of the guards snarled, "You'll do anything we tell you!" and swung at Denbeck, triggering a brawl in his field-level box. Police reinforcements arrived and pummeled the two fans. Meanwhile, next to the melee, a family with several small children was forced to leave because the kids were crying hysterically over the fight.

Denbeck, who lost one of his front teeth in the incident, said the guards threatened to toss him over the railing and down the stairs. Turnbull claimed the guards pounded his head against a wall. Incredibly, even though it was the two fans who were beaten up, they were the ones arrested on assault charges. Another friend, Ed Pietsch, 33, of Richmond Hill, New York, was charged with disorderly conduct and harassment.

"It's unbelievable that they should be charged with assault when they were the ones beaten up," Denbeck's wife, Ellen, told reporters. "I don't think I'll ever go back to Yankee Stadium. We were given mugs [for Fan Appreciation Day] on the way in and we got mugged on the way out."

Scrap Metal Day

Polo Grounds • Sept. 26, 1942

The New York Giants held a "Scrap Metal Day" to help the war effort—but ended up fighting a losing battle at the ball park.

For a doubleheader against the visiting Boston Braves, children were admitted to the Polo Grounds free if they brought some scrap metal for use by the armed forces. More than 11,000 youngsters responded by piling up 56 tons of scrap outside the stadium.

The kids behaved through the first game and most of the nightcap. But in the bottom of the eighth inning, with the home team winning 5–2, the young fans tumbled out of the stands, streamed onto the field, and engulfed the Braves, who were trying to take their positions.

Umpires Ziggy Sears and Tommy Dunn were swallowed in the maelstrom—a hopeless, tangled mass of kids running helter-skelter all over the field. Having fought his way to the Giants dugout, Sears asked for an announcement stating that the game would be forfeited if the field was not cleared. But the announcement couldn't be heard above the din.

The Braves insisted they wanted the game to continue. But city police, special cops, ushers, and grounds crew could not move the wild mob off the field. So, without further ceremony, Sears ordered the game forfeited to Boston, 9–0.

It would have taken a whole Army battalion to round up the rampaging youngsters. But the soldiers overseas had a much bigger fight on their hands.

BALLOT BOX BUNKO

The Most Unconscionable Voting
for Awards and Honors

Tammany Hall and Mayor Richard Daley did not corner the market on voting irregularities. Baseball has endured its share of dirty politics. Whether fans are voting for All-Star teams or sportswriters are selecting MVP awards and Hall of Fame inductees, some results are way off base. For "The Most Unconscionable Voting for Awards and Honors," The Baseball Hall of SHAME inducts the following:

Cincinnati Ballot Box Stuffers

1956 and 1957

Deserving National League players were cheated out of a share of All-Star glory in 1956 and 1957 because of shameless ballot box stuffing perpetrated by Cincinnati Reds fans.

Taking advantage of the ridiculous rule allowing fans to mark as many ballots as they wished, Cincy backers voted repeatedly for their favorites. The fans managed to place five Reds on the starting lineup of the 1956 All-Star team, while three other Cincinnati players were runners-up at their positions.

Spurred on by the exhortations of the Cincinnati news media, the fans tried even harder the following year. In an election scheme that would have embarrassed a banana republic dictator, Cincy fans sent in 550,000 last-minute ballots and elected members of a mediocre Reds team to seven of the eight starting positions for the 1957 All-Star Game. Only Reds left fielder Frank Robinson and Reds catcher Ed Bailey truly deserved to be starters.

The voting was such a travesty that Commissioner Ford Frick finally took action. Citing an "over-balance of Cincinnati ballots," Frick ordered Reds outfielders Gus Bell and Wally Post dropped and replaced with two players who were just a bit more deserving of the honor—Hank Aaron and Willie Mays.

As a result of the Red conspiracy, voting was assigned to the players, managers, and coaches for the next 12 years.

Mel Webb

Sportswriter • *Boston Globe* • Nov. 27, 1947

Mel Webb, a grouchy old scribe for the *Boston Globe*, deliberately bilked Ted Williams out of a justly deserved Most Valuable Player award in 1947.

That year, the Red Sox slugger earned the coveted Triple Crown by batting .343, belting 32 homers, and knocking in 114 RBIs. He was selected "Major League Player of the Year" by *The Sporting News*.

If ever there was a player who deserved to be voted the American League's MVP, it was Williams. Yet he lost out to Yankee outfielder Joe DiMaggio, who batted .315, hit 20 homers, and had 97 RBIs. Good, but not as good as Williams.

Throughout the year, Webb feuded with Williams and wrote nasty articles about the Bosox star. When it came time for sportswriters to vote for MVP honors, Webb flung objectivity aside like a wild pitch. The small-minded writer refused to name Williams even tenth on the ballot, thus throwing the award to DiMaggio by a single point. A tenth-place vote, worth two points, would have been enough to make Williams the league's MVP.

Groused Williams, "The Most Valuable Player award shouldn't depend on being buddy-buddy with a sportswriter." Or on being arch enemies.

Computerized All-Star Ballot

1970–present

The All-Star computerized ballot system has disgraced the mid-season classic. It has made fan voting a mockery.

Because the ballots are printed up before the season starts, rookies and burgeoning new stars are too often left off. Their only hope of starting is through a long-shot, write-in campaign. In 1970, the computerized, pre-printed ballot failed to include either Alex Johnson or Rico Carty, who as regulars the year before had hit .315 and .342 respectively. They wound up as the 1970 batting champs in their respective leagues.

In 1974, White Sox shortstop Luis Aparicio, who had retired prior to the start of the season, was listed on the ballot and received thousands of votes.

The next year's balloting was even more of a joke. Carlton Fisk, who had yet to play a game that year because of an injury, received nearly one million votes. Meanwhile, Red Sox teammate Fred Lynn, who went on to win Rookie of the Year honors and the MVP award, wasn't even on the ballot. Despite a massive write-in effort, Lynn finished fourth among outfielders and didn't start, although he did play. Worse yet, fans that year elected three favorites who were forced to play the wrong positions. Since the ballots were printed before the season started, they did not reflect any of the switches that players had made in their positions from the previous year. As a result, Oakland A's first baseman Joe Rudi played in the outfield, teammate and catcher Gene Tenace played first base, and Reds third baseman Pete Rose played in the outfield.

Since fans can vote as often as they like, the lineups are often influenced by a relatively few people who have nothing better to do than sit around all day punching holes in computer cards. This makes it easy for ignorant fans to elect undeserving players. In 1982, for example, fans allowed Yankee shortstop Bucky Dent, who was batting a sickening .138 at the time, to hold the voting lead until a late surge of ballots elected Brewers shortstop Robin Yount, who became the league's MVP that year.

Is it any wonder that few players base incentive clauses in their contracts on whether or not they make the All-Star team?

Baseball Writers' Association of America Committee on Baseball Veterans

The voters who choose the inductees into The National Baseball Hall of Fame have failed to mete out justice. They have shown a persistent failure to recognize the excellence of dozens of stars who have been passed over for players with much weaker credentials.

Players gain entry into the Hall of Fame through a vote of the Baseball Writers' Association of America. To be eligible, a player must be retired for at least five years. If a deserving player has not been chosen by the writers within a 15-year eligibility period, he must wait an additional three years. He can then be voted in by the Committee on Baseball Veterans—a "court of last resort" composed of players, executives, and sportswriters.

Although they should know better, these judges do not always pay close attention to the record books. For example, here are six former major leaguers with outstanding credentials who have been ignored. Their records cry for recognition:

• Riggs Stephenson (OF-2B, Indians, Cubs, 1921–34)—This awesome line-drive hitter ranks among the top 20 batters of all time. His lifetime batting average of .336 is higher than those of his outfield mates Hack Wilson and Kiki Cuyler, both Hall of Famers.

• Ernie Lombardi (C, Dodgers, Reds, Braves, Giants, 1931–47)—He's the only catcher in the majors to win two batting titles (.342 in 1938 and .330 in 1942), finishing with a career average of .306. An excellent defensive catcher who snap-threw to second base out of a crouch, Lombardi caught 100 or more games in each of 14 consecutive years.

• Carl Mays (P, Red Sox, Yankees, Reds, Giants, 1915–29)—He won 208 games and lost 126 for a phenomenal .623 winning percentage. He also compiled a sparkling 2.92 ERA. A 20-game winner for five seasons, Mays twice led the league in shutouts.

• Richie Ashburn (OF, Phillies, Cubs, Mets, 1948–62)—Twice he was the league batting champion (.338 in 1955 and .350 in 1958). Ashburn's career totals include 2,574 hits and a .308 average. For nine years, Ashburn topped the league in putouts by an outfielder, and for three years he led in assists.

• Pepper Martin (OF-3B, Cardinals, 1928–44)—Pepper excelled when it counted most. His lifetime World Series batting average of .418 is the best in baseball history. A reckless base stealer, he led the league three times in steals. He retired with a .298 lifetime batting average.

• Billy Williams (OF-1B-DH, Cubs, A's, 1959–76)—This iron man played in 1,117 consecutive games, had three seasons of 200 or more hits, and hit 20 or more homers in each of 13 straight years. His lifetime statistics include 2,711 hits, 426 homers, and a .290 batting average.

These and other players have been denied the recognition they deserve. It's an unconscionable blemish on the stature of the Hall of Fame.

WOEFUL WINDUPS

The Most Disastrous Farewell Performances

Careers, franchises, stadiums, and seasons must all come to an end sooner or later. Some bow out gracefully. Others exit without a shred of dignity, leaving behind a residue of shame that even the garbageman won't touch. For "The Most Disastrous Farewell Performances," The Baseball Hall of SHAME inducts the following:

Pittsburgh Pirates' World Championship Reign

Oct. 11, 1972

The world champion Pittsburgh Pirates were just three outs away from winning their second straight National League pennant. But with the title right in their grasp, it was thrown away—on an historic wild pitch.

In the fifth and deciding game of the National League Championship Series in Cincinnati, the Pirates held a razor-thin 3–2 lead over the Reds in the bottom of the ninth inning. With ace reliever Dave Giusti on the mound, Pittsburgh could already taste the champagne.

But on this day, of all days, Giusti didn't have his stuff. He gave up a dramatic game-tying homer and back-to-back singles before right-hander Bob Moose, normally a starting pitcher, relieved him. Moose retired the next batter on a long fly that advanced runner George Foster to third base—only 90 feet away from the title. Moose bore down and coaxed a pop-up. Now there were two outs. To send the game into extra innings, Moose desperately needed to retire hitter Hal McRae.

The count went to 1-and-1. Then Moose threw a hard slider down and away—but a little too down and a little too far away. The ball skipped into the dirt to the right of home plate and bounced over catcher Manny Sanguillen's head. The catcher frantically retrieved the ball, but it was much too late. Foster had already raced across the plate with the pennant-winning run. There was nothing Sanguillen could do but fling the ball into center field in a final gesture of frustration over the inglorious end to the Pirates' reign as world champs.

Fred Lindstrom's Career

April 16, 1936

Future Hall of Famer Fred Lindstrom knew it was time to quit the game after enduring the most embarrassing moment of his career.

Lindstrom, once the Giant third baseman recognized as the finest this side of Pie Traynor, was playing left field for the Dodgers at the Polo Grounds against his old New York team. Brooklyn was winning 6–5, with two out in the bottom of the ninth. Giant runners Mel Ott and Burgess Whitehead were on first and second base when batter Hank Leiber hit a high pop-up to short left field.

Lindstrom flipped down his sunglasses and charged in while shortstop Jimmy Jordan raced out. "I got it!" yelled Lindstrom. "I'll take it!" shouted Jordan. "Who's got it?" asked both.

As the ball plopped into Jordan's glove, the onrushing Lindstrom crashed into him, causing the ball to pop out and roll away. By the time it was retrieved, both Ott and Whitehead had raced home with the tying and winning runs for a lucky 7–6 Giant victory.

Afterward, in the losers' silent clubhouse, Lindstrom told his teammates, "I never thought it would happen to me. I'll tell you this, it's never going to happen again."

The incident preyed heavily on his mind. A month later, the 13-year veteran quit the team and retired from baseball.

AP/Wide World Photo

New York Mets' Loss

Sept. 11, 1974

For a torturous seven hours and four minutes, the Mets battled the Cardinals in a 25-inning marathon that lasted so late even the night crawlers were asleep.

Only 1,000 diehard fans from the original Shea Stadium crowd of 13,460 stuck by their team until the final out at 3:13 A.M. in the longest night game in major league history.

So how did the Mets reward their fans' loyalty and staying power? New York blew the game on a play that would make a Little Leaguer wince.

The score was tied 3–3 in the top of the 25th inning when Met pitcher Hank Webb tried to pick Bake McBride off first base. The ball sailed past first baseman John Milner and bounded into right field foul territory. McBride raced all the way to third and, deciding there was no sense stopping at that late hour, came charging home like an express train. He should have been derailed at the plate; Milner's throw to catcher Ron Hodges arrived in plenty of time for the out. But Hodges dropped the ball. McBride scored the winning run in the marathon game courtesy of two Met errors on the same play.

WGRZ-TV's Telecast of Nolan Ryan's No-Hitter

Sept. 26, 1981

In the most deplorable ending to a baseball telecast, Buffalo, New York station WGRZ-TV pulled the plug on viewers watching an unparalleled fifth no-hitter by Nolan Ryan.

It was a shameful reminder of the infamous "Heidi" game on November 17, 1968. Remember? The New York Jets were beating the Oakland Raiders 32–29 with 61 seconds left in the nationally-televised football game when NBC cut away to show its scheduled special, "Heidi." Outraged viewers missed seeing the Raiders' dramatic two-touchdown comeback to win the thriller 43–32.

Thirteen years later, TV watchers were once again left dangling in suspense. Only this time the viewers were those who turned to Buffalo's Channel 2 (then known as WRG-TV, an NBC affiliate).

After showing the entire game between the Detroit Tigers and the Milwaukee Brewers on *NBC's Game of the Week*, the station picked up the telecast of the network's backup game, in which Houston Astros hurler Nolan Ryan was no-hitting the Los Angeles Dodgers. At the end of eight innings, the Astros, battling for first place in the pennant race, were winning 5–0. Ryan had struck out 10 and walked three. Could he pitch another no-hitter?

As Channel 2 viewers edged closer to their TV screens for the start of the crucial ninth inning, disaster struck. The station suddenly broke away from the exciting finish and switched to its originally-scheduled programming. The stunned and angry viewers missed seeing Ryan mow down the last three Dodger batters with a strikeout and two groundouts to make baseball history.

Just what was so important that the station had to preempt the finale to Ryan's masterpiece, causing irate TV watchers to flood the station with calls of protest? Channel 2 felt duty-bound to present a naval training film—*Life Aboard an Aircraft Carrier.*

Red Barber's Yankee Broadcasting Job

Sept. 26, 1966

Red Barber, who spent 13 illustrious years at a Yankee microphone, was callously fired—because he reported the truth.

It happened just days after the 1966 Yankees—a pathetic team that wound up in last place for the first time in half a century—were playing a meaningless, late-season home game against the Chicago White Sox. Only the most diehard fans were there, all 413 of them. It was the worst attendance ever at Yankee Stadium.

In the broadcast booth, Barber asked for a camera shot of the 59,597 empty seats. He felt such a picture would be an eloquent commentary on the end of the great Yankee dynasty. But Perry Smith, the club's vice president for radio and television, had ordered the cameramen not to show the seats. They weren't even allowed to follow a foul ball into the stands or down the foul lines.

Barber, a respected major league baseball announcer for 33 consecutive years, considered himself a reporter above all else. He wouldn't be cowed. Denied pictures, he told the story in words.

"I don't know what the paid attendance is today," he told his audience. "But whatever it is, it's the smallest crowd in the history of the stadium. And this smallest crowd is the story, not the ball game."

Four days later, Michael Burke, who had been installed as president of the Yankees less than a week earlier, summoned Barber to a breakfast meeting in the Edwardian Room of the Plaza Hotel.

Barber later told reporters, "I thought he was going to say I could help the Yankees; that my great experience was surely one of the things the Yankees could depend upon. I thought he was going to say that I was a well-known figure; that I was a leader in civic organizations; that I was a personality that he would call on time and time again to help this bad ball club. I thought he was going to, but he didn't.

"I gave him a sports book and said there was some good writing in it. A pleasantry. And he said to me: 'There's no sense in talking like that. We have decided not to renew your contract.' Needless to say, I didn't order breakfast."

In sacking a great broadcaster, Burke had reverted to ancient ways. Amid the ruins of a fallen empire, Burke had disposed of the messenger who brought bad news.

Los Angeles Angels' Loss

Aug. 16, 1961

The Los Angeles Angels literally threw a game away on a final play that didn't even belong on a sandlot.

The visiting Angels were trying to hang on to a 2–1 lead in the bottom of the ninth inning in a game against the Washington Senators. In a last-ditch rally, the Senators, with two outs, had runners Bud Zipfel and Marty Keough on first and second repsectively.

The next batter, Jim King, hit a routine grounder to Eddie Yost at third base. Angels manager Bill Rigney smiled and clapped his hands in celebration of an expected victory as Yost effortlessly fielded the ball for what appeared to be the last out of the game.

Unfortunately, the third sacker threw wildly past second baseman Rocky Bridges and blew the force-out; the ball sailed into right field as Keough scored the tying run. Rigney groaned in dismay, but the worst was yet to come.

Right fielder Albie Pearson scooped up the errant throw—and then fired one of his own. Trying to nail Zipfel at third, Pearson pegged the ball over Yost's head and right between the legs of pitcher Jim Donahue, who was backing up the play. Zipfel then trotted home with the winning run.

Meanwhile, the ball bounded into the Angels dugout and landed right on Rigney's lap. Angrily, he held the ball so tight, that his knuckles turned white. Then he shoved it in his pocket, mumbling, "I'm going to keep this ball so it can't do any more damage."

The All-Time Baseball Hall of SHAME De-Meritorious Award

As great a game as baseball is, its reputation as America's pastime has been sullied by a myth that has lingered for many years. Although baseball has overcome scandals, strikes, and Bowie Kuhn, it has failed to rid itself of a deplorable age-old blight—the shame of shames. For this reason, The Baseball Hall of SHAME presents a special dishonor to the following:

A. G. Spalding
Sporting Goods Magnate

Stephen Clark
Millionaire

Kenesaw Mountain Landis
Commissioner of Baseball

The story that Abner Doubleday scratched out the design for a game on the Cooperstown village green in 1839 and thus invented baseball is a two-base falsehood.

He had nothing to do with the founding of baseball. And neither did Cooperstown. The tale was just part of a conspiracy to sell more sporting equipment, boost tourism, and promote baseball.

At the turn of the century, sporting goods magnate A. G. Spalding was determined to prove that baseball had been invented in America despite clear evidence that it had evolved from the British games of rounders and cricket. He reasoned that more Americans would buy his baseball equipment if they believed the game was born in the USA.

In 1905, Spalding appointed a six-man commission to determine the game's true origin. But he wasn't about to let truth stand in the way of profit. He stacked the commission not with skilled investigators but with baseball men who were out to prove by hook or by crook that baseball was 100 percent American.

On December 30, 1907, the Spalding Commission reported that baseball was invented by Abner Doubleday in Cooperstown, New York, in 1839. The decision was based entirely on a letter from 73-year-old Abner Graves, who would later end up in an asylum for the criminally insane. Graves claimed that 68 years earlier in Cooperstown, in the summer of 1839, he saw his boyhood pal Doubleday use a stick to draw up plans in the dirt for a new game called baseball.

Balderdash! In 1839, Graves was only five years old; Doubleday was nearly 20. At that time, Doubleday was a cadet at West Point, and no record exists of his leaving the academy that summer. Besides, his family had moved out of Cooperstown two years earlier.

Furthermore, Doubleday, who became a general and Civil War hero at Gettysburg, never tried to take credit for inventing baseball. After retiring from the Army in 1873, he published many articles and left 67 diaries. None mention baseball.

Doubleday couldn't refute the baseball lie because he had died in 1893, 14 years before he was officially named the game's founder.

The Spalding Commission report might have languished forgotten in some filing cabinet had it not been for Cooperstown millionaire Stephen Clark. He decided the Doubleday tall tale might be a good hustle for suckering tourists into the isolated village. So, in 1935, he launched his scheme to establish a national baseball museum.

Clark had no trouble selling the idea to baseball's bigwigs. After all, they were hurting at the turnstiles from the Depression, and were looking for new ways to promote the game. They went along with the deception and even planned a season-long celebration for baseball's "centennial" in 1939. Anything for a buck.

The National Baseball Hall of Fame and Museum was established in 1939 in Cooperstown, with honors bestowed posthumously upon Abner Doubleday. Had the powers that be been true to the game, they would have built the shrine at the birthplace of modern baseball—Hoboken, New Jersey. And they would have honored the real originator of modern baseball—Alexander Cartwright, Jr.

Commissioner Kenesaw Mountain Landis knew the truth about the origin of the sport but swept it aside. Before the "centennial," Landis received a letter from Bruce Cartwright, who documented the fact that it was his grandfather, Alexander Cartwright, Jr., and not Doubleday, who drew out the first baseball diamond and wrote the rules. It's a matter of record that Alexander Cartwright, who headed a rules committee in 1845, established the foul lines, set the distance between the bases at 90 feet, and fixed the number of players on a side at nine.

The first game of baseball under the Cartwright rules was played on June 19, 1846, on the old cricket grounds at Elysian Fields, a summer resort in Hoboken, New Jersey. The Knickerbocker Baseball Club (of which Cartwright was a charter member) lost to the New York Club 23–1 in a four-inning game.

Landis chose to ignore these facts. Cartwright's grandson Bruce died a few weeks after writing to Landis, and the letter was filed away. Too much money and prestige had been committed for the lords of baseball to be bothered by facts.

Today, the only official recognition of Cartwright is a plaque at The Baseball Hall of Fame and Museum identifying him simply as "*a* father of modern baseball."

The conspirators won. Spalding boosted sales of baseball equipment, Cooperstown's coffers began filling up with tourists' money, and baseball promoted its mythical roots.

Meanwhile, Abner Doubleday remains the unfounded father of baseball.

WHO ELSE BELONGS
IN THE
BASEBALL HALL OF SHAME?

Do you have any nominations for The Baseball Hall of SHAME? Give us your picks for the most shameful, embarrassing, deplorable, blundering, and boneheaded moments in baseball history. Here's your opportunity to pay a light-hearted tribute to the game we all love.

On separate sheets of paper, describe your nominations in detail. Those nominations that are documented with the greatest number of facts, such as first-hand accounts, newspaper or magazine clippings, box scores, or photos have the best chance of being inducted into The Baseball Hall of SHAME. Feel free to send as many nominations as you wish. If you don't find an existing category listed in our Baseball Hall of SHAME books that fits your nomination, then make up your own category. (All submitted material becomes the property of The Baseball Hall of SHAME and is nonreturnable.) Mail your nominations to:

The Baseball Hall of SHAME
P.O. Box 6218
West Palm Beach, FL 33405

THE WINNING
TEAM

The establishment of The Baseball Hall of SHAME is the realization of a lifelong dream for its two founders:

Bruce Nash has felt the sting of baseball shame ever since he smashed a sure triple in a Pee Wee League game and was almost thrown out at first base because he was so slow afoot. He graduated to Little League but "played" his first and only season without ever swinging at a pitch. His most embarrassing moment on the field occurred in a sandlot game when a misjudged fly ball bounced off his head allowing the winning run to score. As a die-hard Dodger fan in Brooklyn, Nash was so traumatized by the team's surprise departure that he ended up rooting for the Yankees.

Allan Zullo is an expert on losers. He rooted for the Chicago Cubs during their long cellar-dwelling years. Playing baseball throughout his childhood, he patterned himself after his Cub heroes. That explains why his longest hit in the Pony League was a pop fly double that the first baseman lost in the sun. As a park league coach, Zullo achieved the distinction of piloting a team that did not hit a fair ball in either game of a double-header. Unaccustomed to the Cubs' extraordinary success in 1984, Zullo has switched allegiances—to the Cleveland Indians.

Compiling and maintaining records is the most important task of the Hall's curator, **Bernie Ward**. His baseball days during his childhood followed a consistent and predictable pattern—consistently awful and predictably short. His teammates called him "the executioner" because he killed so many of his team's rallies by striking out or hitting into inning-ending double plays.